# THE DOORS OF TAROT

# THE DOORS OF TAROT

## Lessons for the Practical Diviner

*John Gilbert*
*Edited by John Michael Greer*

**AEON**

First published in 2023 by
Aeon Books

Copyright © 2023 by John Gilbert

British Library Cataloguing in Publication Data

A C.I.P. for this book is available from the British Library

ISBN-13: 978-1-80152-077-5

Typeset by Medlar Publishing Solutions Pvt Ltd, India

www.aeonbooks.co.uk

# CONTENTS

# INTRODUCTION

I met John Gilbert for the first time at a tarot conference in Portland, Oregon over Labor Day weekend in 2001. The Pacific Northwest has a reputation for gray skies and heavy rains, but that weekend did its best to convince us all otherwise: the sun shone, the skies were luminous blue, and the hills around the hotel where we were meeting were vivid with evergreens. It was a propitious time for one of the most important encounters in my spiritual life.

John and I had been exchanging emails by then for most of a year, partly about the tarot, partly about other mutual interests, of which we had plenty. I'd seen photos of him by then, but when we met in person I was bowled over by the intensity of the man. Tall and genial, he carried his sixty-three years lightly and radiated a sense of calm acceptance of whatever the universe could throw at him. Fifteen minutes after our first meeting we were chatting like old friends.

We only met in person two times after that, both of them at weekend events, but for more than a decade we kept the internet and the phone lines humming with emails and calls. Most of those focused on subjects unrelated to the tarot. Our great project was the revival of the Ancient Order of Druids in America (AODA), of which John was one of the last living initiates, but I also studied and received initiation and consecration into the other esoteric traditions he had received from his teachers—the Universal Gnostic Church, the Order of Spiritual Alchemy, the Magickal Order of the Golden Dawn, and the Modern Order of Essenes. Over the course of our friendship, I got to know a fair amount about the man.

John Gilbert was born in 1938 in Pierre, South Dakota, and moved to Colorado with his family in his teens. He was an Eagle Scout and an honor student, as well as an enthusiastic athlete, setting state records in track and field. As soon as he graduated from high school he left home and joined the Coast Guard, then used his GI Bill benefits to attend college and take up a career as a high school teacher. While in college, he married his first wife, Judith.

It was at some point in the 1960s—John never mentioned the date to me—that he met his occult teacher, Rev. Matthew Shaw. Shaw was a minister of the Universalist Church who left that denomination in 1952, as it moved toward a merger with the Unitarians. With two other former Universalist clergymen, Shaw founded a new denomination, the Universal Gnostic Church and embarked on a pilgrimage across the landscape of American alternative spirituality. By the time John met him, Shaw went by the name Rhodonn Starrus—"Rose Cross" in Greek—and had joined forces with another remarkable figure of the time, Dr. Juliet Ashley, a student of Carl Jung and Edgar Cayce. In the course of his training with Shaw and Ashley, John was introduced to the tarot cards.

The rest, as they say, was history.

John was an extraordinarily capable tarot diviner, and he also drew on his experience as a high school teacher to become an even more extraordinary teacher of tarot. He loved to give workshops in which a roomful of complete beginners would pick up a tarot deck for the first time and be able to read the cards accurately and easily in a single day. Where most tarot readers and teachers focus on multiple-card readings, John always encouraged students to get as much as they could out of a single card. He used to do single-card readings at tarot and metaphysical events that astounded people for their clarity and accuracy.

Over the years that followed, John was involved in various organizations in the alternative spirituality scene, including several focused on the tarot. His abilities as an organizer and manager were not always up to the same high level as his talents as a teacher and diviner, however, and he fell afoul more than once of the bitter internal politics that so often plague small groups. It was after one such debacle that he founded a small organization of his own, the Tarot Institute, and set out to transform his most successful workshops into weekly lessons that could be sent to subscribers over the internet. Most of those lessons are collected in this book; the remaining lessons, which deal with issues of spirituality and philosophy rather than tarot divination, are included in another volume, *The Tree of Spirit*.

The first chapter of this book has been assembled from introductory essays on the Tarot Institute website. Each of the remaining chapters was a separate course offered by the Tarot Institute, and each of the lessons was meant to be studied for a week, so there is a certain amount of unavoidable overlap from course to course. I have done only minimal editing, so that John's voice can come through the lessons as clearly as possible.

The Tarot Institute was one of John's later projects, and it found only a modest audience. Toward the end of his life, frustrated by a series of similar disappointments, he withdrew from teaching, and finally he and his second wife Charlene moved to Laramie, Wyoming so he could be close to his children in his last years. He died there early in 2021. I am honored to be able to help get his writings into print so that those who didn't have the chance to meet John Gilbert can still have the opportunity to learn from him.

— John Michael Greer

## CHAPTER 1

# First steps in tarot

### How tarot cards work

Our subconscious mind thinks in symbols. It's in communication with the Spiritual Universe along with everybody else's subconscious mind. Our conscious mind thinks in words. It's in tune with the physical world along with most other people on this planet. Tarot cards are composed of a group of symbols which we define in words. Therefore, tarot cards can be a tool to help our subconscious mind communicate with our conscious mind. Since our subconscious mind is in communication with every other subconscious mind, we can actually use tarot cards to help other people learn about themselves.

At least that's one theory about how tarot cards work. It's the theory I accept because it proves itself to me over and over every day of my life. I can't ever remember when the cards lied to me about anything. I've done my share of misinterpreting the cards, but that's my problem. But as far as I know, the cards have always been honest and forthright with me about everything.

My suggestion is to accept the theory being proposed and give it a try. If it works for you, keep on believing and reading. If it doesn't work for you, try something else, some other theory. My guess is it'll work just fine for you but sometimes guesses can be wrong.

## What tarot symbols mean

Has it ever bothered you that several authors, all looking at the same symbols in the same cards, give several different meanings for those symbols? That used to bother me. In fact, I used to agree with some authors and think the other authors were all wrong. I even remember correcting tarot readers for misinterpreting a card or telling them what a particular card really meant. In this way I announced my own ignorance. I'm sure the readers weren't all that happy about doing a reading for me.

The truth is all those authors were correct. Those symbols mean exactly what they say the symbols mean—at least to them. When they're reading the symbols their meaning is the one that counts. When I'm reading the symbols, my meaning is the one that counts. When you're reading the symbols, your meaning is the one that counts. Each of us interprets different symbols in different ways because of who we are, what we know, what we think we know, and what we've experienced in our life.

Today when somebody does a reading for me, I listen to what they say about the cards. I listen to the meanings they attach to the symbols. I don't judge them or any meanings they assign to any symbols. I listen and strive to understand. I can't begin to tell you how much more I get out of a tarot reading today. I'm sure the readers appreciate not being told "the right way to do it."

## The meanings of the tarot cards

Tarot cards mean to us exactly what they mean, no more and no less. When you look at a card and get a feeling about what a certain symbol means, my suggestion is to write it down and remember that. Keep a book of notes about the cards, one page for each card. Review these notes on a regular basis until both your conscious and subconscious mind know and understand what each card means to you, what each symbol on each card means to you. That's my suggestion.

Good tarot readers are good because they know what each card means and they know what the major symbols in each card mean. Their subconscious mind chooses the right card at the right time to communicate precisely what needs to be communicated then. Their subconscious mind will draw their eyes to the correct symbol within each card to communicate the message that needs to be received now.

Every tarot author has his or her own opinions about what each card means. You can use these meanings if you want to use them. You can use another author's opinion for any deck you choose to use. You can also make up your own meanings.

One way to decide what each tarot card means is to keep a notebook and write down every meaning given by every author in every tarot book you read. Another way to decide is to write down only those meanings you like for each card. You can also select meanings that are easy to remember when you look at the card. The secret is that the tarot cards mean exactly what you decide they mean. Of course, you can always memorize the meanings given by the author of your choice. That may sound like the easy way out, but in my experience it's a more difficult task—unless the key words are printed on the cards.

You'll either make this decision consciously or unconsciously. If you make a conscious decision, you'll better understand the process and probably become a talented tarot reader. If you do it unconsciously, you'll always be in the dark wondering if you're doing it right or not.

Here's the process I suggest:

1. Keep a tarot notebook with one page dedicated to each card
2. Write down all the meanings you select for each card
3. Choose one meaning, one key word or phrase for each card
4. Read this meaning over and over so your subconscious mind knows too
5. Make up a "cheat sheet" and do practice readings
6. When you know the meanings for most of the cards most of the time join a free tarot reading group and start doing readings
7. When you know and understand your cards, start reading for money
8. Change the meaning you use for any card any time
9. Just be certain your subconscious mind knows about the change too

The meanings of the tarot cards are exactly those meanings you and your subconscious mind agree upon. You make the decision and tell your subconscious mind this is the definition for this card. Once you've done this, the responsibility for choosing the correct card for any reading is up to your subconscious mind. Since your subconscious mind is infallible, it'll always choose the right card. Then it's your responsibility to remember what that card means and interpret it in the reading. That's what the meaning of the tarot cards is all about.

## Clearing your tarot cards

It is important to clear negative energy from your tarot decks before you use them, and there are several ways of doing this. These same techniques can be used for removing negative energy from crystals, amulets, talismans, bracelets, brooches, necklaces, magical tools, ceremonial weapons, and other personal or spiritual articles. The instructions given will usually work with one application of the technique.

The first method I want to discuss here is elemental clearing or cleansing. This is accomplished using symbols chosen to represent the elements of Earth, Water, Fire, and Air. The usual symbols are given in this chapter but readers are encouraged to use any similar materials in their own clearing rituals. Clearing with Spirit is called Consecration and will be covered later in this chapter. Clearing with Elemental Weapons is also a form of Consecration.

As a rule, you'll find it easier to clear and cleanse your deck of unwanted negative energies by fanning the deck open and doing the whole deck at once when using Water, Fire, and Air Elemental Cleansing techniques. If extreme cleansing is needed, the cards can be cleared one at a time. As a rule only one form of Elemental Clearing is used. However, readers are encouraged to be creative and use as many elements as desired.

When the allotted period of time expires, check your tarot deck to see if it still exudes any negative energy. If it does, or if in doubt about the outcome, repeat the process as many times as required to clear the deck of all negative energy. When you're done with the cleansing, dispose of the materials used for the cleansing.

## Earth Elemental Clearing

1. Bury your protected deck in sand, salt, or dirt for twenty-four hours.
2. Fan your deck open on a tablecloth and sprinkle it with salt and/or sand, and leave it for one to two minutes.
3. Fan your deck as above but instead of salt and/or sand, use any combination of any of the following herbs: basil, lavender, rosemary, sage, thyme, the crushed dried leaves of any plant or tree, or the crushed dried flowers of any plant.

4. Rub your deck for a minute or two with any of these materials.
5. Place your deck under your pillow or mattress and sleep on it overnight.

## Water Elemental Clearing

1. Sprinkle your cards lightly with water. Wipe immediately.
2. Sprinkle your cards with salt water (1 tablespoon salt to 1 cup water). Wipe immediately.
3. Sprinkle your cards with consecrated water. Wipe immediately.
4. Sprinkle your cards with any herbal tea or plant infusion. Wipe immediately.
5. Expose your deck to moonlight in a protected area for half the night.

## Fire Elemental Clearing

1. Pass your deck quickly through a candle flame. Don't burn yourself.
2. Place your deck on a table with a candle holder and lighted candle on it for five minutes.
3. Place your deck on a table with a candle and aromatic oil diffuser for five minutes.
4. Expose your deck to sunlight in a protected area for half a day.

## Air Elemental Clearing

1. Pass your deck five to seven times over burning incense.
2. Smudge your deck with sage or any similar smudge.
3. Take a deep breath and breathe deeply and slowly into your deck three times.
4. Place your deck on a cassette or video player playing good music for one hour.

## Cleansing by consecration

Consecration is an intention to make a person, place, or thing holy. By making it holy all negativity is completely and instantly removed from the person, place, or thing. Intention is the most important ingredient in any consecration. If you intend to bless, clear, cleanse, and consecrate a person, place, or thing, and your intention is sincere, then the consecration occurs just as you intend it.

Consecration is usually done in a reverent manner, preceded by prayers of invocation, thanksgiving, and petition. Invocation is a prayer asking Deity, by whatever name you wish to use, to assist in the intended ceremony. Thanksgiving is a prayer thanking Deity for one's life, blessings, gifts, health, family, friends, and happiness. Petition is a prayer asking for something. Be careful, prayers of petition are not begging for fame and fortune. They're prayers asking for forgiveness, assistance, knowledge, and blessing.

To consecrate a tarot deck, first decide what purpose the deck is to serve. Divination, meditation, visualization, and spiritual advancement are typical purposes for a tarot deck. Prepare yourself and your spiritual altar for the ceremony. Invoke the Deity of your choice and inform this Deity of your intention in regards to the tarot deck. Ask Deity to assist you in performing the ceremony and accomplishing your intention.

The next step is to recite whatever prayers of petition and thanksgiving you want to use. Following these prayers is the consecration ceremony. This can be as simple as: "In the name of (name of Deity) I hereby bless, clear, cleanse, charge, and consecrate you to be (blank) for the purpose of (blank)." Fill in the blanks according to your intention and purpose for this deck.

## Cleansing with Elemental Weapons

Elemental Weapons are special implements consecrated to be the representative for a particular element. There are some usual correspondences, but readers are encouraged to make and consecrate their own Elemental Weapons of their choice. The usual correspondences are:

Air – Sword or Dagger
Water – Cup or Chalice
Fire – Wand or Spear
Earth – Pentacle or Disk

Cleansing with an Elemental Weapon is usually done in a formal ritual but this is not required. Any formal ritual may be used including Wiccan, Christian, Buddhist, Golden Dawn, Masonic, or Rosicrucian ritual. Any informal ritual may also be used. The form used is entirely up to the reader and may include Invocation of Deity, Prayer of Thanksgiving, Prayers of Cleansing and Consecration, and closing prayers.

The ritual may include representatives of any of the elements such as salt or sand, incense, candles, and a chalice filled with water, wine, or juice. During the ceremony the deck is normally touched by one or more of the Elemental Weapons accompanied with words of blessing, clearing, cleansing, charging, and consecration.

## Other cleansing methods

*Using a spiritual space*: Placing your deck on your spiritual altar for a day or two can achieve the same purpose. This may sound strange, but readers who use this approach say it helps to inform your altar of the purpose for placing the deck there. By simply saying: "I'm placing this tarot deck in this holy space for the purpose of removing all negativity from it," the process seems to work better.

My personal feeling about this is that holy space is closely aligned with Deity. Whatever you say to Deity or this holy space will be heard by the elementals, nature spirits, and angels assigned to that space. Since these beings all want to work with humanity, it's just natural for them to clear and cleanse any object you place on your altar. By stating your purpose in doing so you remove all ambiguity and give the elementals, nature spirits, and angels some guidance according to your desires. Ask and it shall be given unto you.

If you regularly clear and cleanse yourself from all negativity or place a sphere of protection around yourself, you're a walking spiritual space yourself. You can keep your tarot deck in your aura for a period of time in order to cleanse and clear it of all negativity. You can accomplish the same goal by placing a personal amulet on top of the deck. A personal amulet is a pocket object or totem you carry with you for some purpose such as protection.

You can create a spiritual space anywhere you want by consecrating that space. You could use a drawer, a table or furniture top, a room or a space outside in the yard or garden. Consecrate this space and place your deck there for a day. Again, it helps to let this space know the purpose of leaving the deck there. I also like to announce for how long the deck or object will remain in this place. Usually it's one day but, if the object is really negatively charged, I'll leave it there for a week or even longer.

*Using a spiritual object*: You can rest your deck on a table or in a drawer with any spiritual object of your choice. If you don't already have a few spiritual objects on your altar, you can consecrate one and use it with your tarot deck. Telling your spiritual object the purpose for leaving it with your tarot deck really seems to speed up the process.

I usually have one or more amulets of protection, love, and peace available for this purpose. I also use spiritual objects from my spiritual altar from time to time. It doesn't matter what the object is. What matters is the purpose for which that object was consecrated. For example, an abundance wand may not be the best object to use for removing negative energies. Objects used for blessing, protection, clearing, cleansing, and consecration generally work the best in my opinion.

## In closing …

As with most things spiritual, your intention is the most important part of the ritual or ceremony. Be very clear about your intention in regards to any objects you wish to clear and cleanse. Voice these intentions out loud so all your spirit guides, angels, nature spirits, and elementals know your intentions regarding the object to be cleared. Expect good things to happen and they will.

CHAPTER 2

# Beginning tarot readings

This chapter is based on a course, Easy Tarot, that taught thousands of complete beginners how to do tarot divination in one day. There are seven sections and each section is designed to take you about one half hour to complete. In addition to this chapter, you'll need to complete the second chapter on one-card tarot readings before you can use your tarot deck—but once you do this, you'll be doing clear, accurate readings with the tarot, and you can build on that foundation to learn more detailed ways of reading the cards.

1

Select the aces and Key I (usually The Magician) from your tarot deck and place these five cards in a row in front of you. You're going to do two things with these cards. The first thing is to define the elements of these five cards. You can refer to the previous chapter to define these elements. You can use any definition you want. Or, you can use the following definitions I'm going to use as an example for these lessons: Swords = Air = thoughts and ideas, Cups = Water = relationships, Wands = Fire = career and work, Pentacles = Earth = financial affairs, and Spirit = spiritual path or the point which needs to be addressed on the client's spiritual path (or my path if I'm the client). I'll use these definitions for examples. You're free to use them or any other set of definitions you want to use.

My only suggestion regarding assigning meaning to the elements, and thus to the suits, is to use one and only one key word, phrase, or concept for each card. The more meanings you assign to cards, especially in the beginning, the more confusing your readings will be. You won't know when to use what meaning with which card. By limiting yourself to one key word, phrase, or concept, you eliminate this possibility.

It doesn't matter what key word, phrase, or concept you decide to assign to each element. What matters is that you define the elements and assign some meaning to each one of them. It matters because whatever you decide will be shared with your subconscious mind and your subconscious mind will use those definitions as it selects the cards for you to do your readings. You won't be conscious of this process, but your subconscious mind knows what it's doing and it will always select the right card according to the definitions it thinks you're using at the time. So be specific. Let your subconscious mind know what meanings you assign to the five elements and five suits of your deck.

The second thing you're going to do with these five cards is assign a meaning to the number one. In the Easy Tarot we assign the first thing a child does, besides cry and eliminate waste, to the aces and Key I. Think about a child. What can a child do besides, eat, cry, and eliminate waste? What's the first thing a child does?

The first thing a child does, and the first thing all of us do when we encounter a new situation, is to pay attention to what's happening. We pay attention to become aware. We must be aware we can change something before we can change it. We must be aware we can do something before we can do it. We must be aware we can learn something before we can learn it.

To become aware, to pay attention, is what the aces and The Magician are all about. The key phrase I assign to The Magician and four aces is to "Pay attention." Pay attention to your spiritual path (Key I). Pay attention to your thoughts and ideas (Ace of Swords). Pay attention to your relationships (Ace of Cups). Pay attention to your career (Ace of Wands). Pay attention to your finances (Ace of Pentacles). Pay attention. If two or more aces or one appear in your spread, that means to *really* pay attention!

That's the first two steps: 1) define the elements, and 2) define the number one.

Put those five cards aside and pick out the four twos and Key II from your deck. Place them in front of you in a row so you can see all five cards. Remember what definitions you assigned to the five elements and suits. Aside from that, the only thing you need to do with these cards is to define the meaning of the number two.

In the Easy Tarot we assign the second thing a child learns to do to The High Priestess (or Key II) and the twos. It's the second thing we all do when we find ourselves in a strange situation. First we pay attention and then we remember what we did before in similar situations, we remember the people, places, and things we've seen before. This act of remembering is the second thing we do.

The key word I assign to The High Priestess and four twos is "Remember" and the key phrase is "Remember the past." Remember your spiritual path, the one you've already chosen (Spirit). Remember your thoughts and ideas (Air). Remember your relationships (Water). Remember your career (Fire). Remember your finances (Earth). Remember the mistakes and the good times of the past. Remembering these things is important at this time. As soon as you know the Keys I and II and the aces and twos, you may proceed to the next section.

## 2

Select the five threes from your deck, including Key III and spread them out in front of you. Review the meanings you've assigned to the five elements. Consider the third thing a child does as it becomes aware of its new world. Consider the third thing we all do when confronting a new situation. First we and the child pay attention and then we all remember something from our past that applies to the new situation.

The third thing a child does, and the third thing we all do in new circumstances, is to imagine future possible outcomes based on our current situation. Imagining future outcomes is the third thing we learn to do as a child and it's the third thing we do in any new situation. In the Easy Tarot we assign the key phrase "Imagine the possibilities" and the key word "Imagination" to The Empress (Key III) and the threes in the tarot deck. Imagine the possibilities of your spiritual path, your finances, your career, your relationships, and your thoughts and ideas. Decide what key word or phrase you want to use with the number three.

Set these five cards aside, select the five fours and place them in a row in front of you. The fourth thing a child does and the fourth thing we do when we're in a strange situation is to reason things out for ourselves. We think things through for ourselves. This act of reasoning is the fourth mental skill we develop as a child. In the Easy Tarot we assign the key phrase "Reason things out for yourself" and the key word "Think!" to The Emperor and the fours of our tarot deck. Think about your spiritual path, your thoughts and ideas, your relationships, your career, and your finances. Decide what key word or phrase you want to use with the number four.

Set these cards aside, select the five fives and place them in a row in front of you. The fifth thing a child does and the fifth thing we do in a strange situation is to rely on our intuitive insights. Intuition is the fifth mental skill we develop as a child. In the Easy Tarot we assign the key phrase "Expect and anticipate intuitive insights" and the key word "Intuition" to The Hierophant and the fives of the tarot deck. Use your intuition regarding your finances, your career, your relationship, your thoughts and ideas, and your spiritual path. Decide what key word or phrase you want to use with the number five.

When you've learned Keys III, IV, and V and the threes, fours, and fives, you're ready to go on to the next section.

## 3

Select the sixes, sevens, and eights from your tarot deck including Keys VI, VII, and VIII. Spread the sixes and Key VI out in front of you. Review the meanings you've assigned to the five elements, the five suits.

The sixth mental skill a child develops after they pay attention, remember, imagine, reason, and intuit is their conscience, their ability to distinguish between right and wrong, good and bad. This skill is called discrimination in alchemy and by the mystery schools. In the Easy Tarot we assign the key phrase of "Listen to your conscience" and the key word "Discriminate" to the sixes in the tarot deck. Listen to your conscience regarding your spiritual path, regarding your finances, regarding your relationships, regarding your career, and regarding your thoughts and ideas. Decide what key word or phrase you want to use with the number six.

Set these cards aside and spread the sevens including Key VII before you. The last mental skill a child develops is the skill of being receptive.

This is also the highest mental skill of an adult. In the Easy Tarot we use the key phrase "Be receptive to divine influence" and the key word "Be receptive" to the sevens of the tarot deck. Be receptive to divine influence in your finances, your career, your relationships, your thoughts and ideas, and your spiritual path. Decide what key word or phrase you want to use with the number seven. Set these cards aside.

This completes our discussion of childhood and basic mental skills. We now move into adolescence and the development of abstract thought. Before we can think in abstract terms we must have well-developed mental skills as outlined in the first seven numbers. Before we can think in higher spiritual terms we must develop our abstract thinking skills.

Spread the eights including Key VIII in front of you. We're going to consider first the possibility where Strength is the eighth Key as this is the most common assignment in modern tarot decks. This card tells us we have the inner strength to accomplish whatever we set our minds to accomplish. All we have to have is the intention to do it, the belief we can do it and the determination to do it. In the Easy Tarot we assign the key concept "You have the inner strength to accomplish …" and the key phrase "You can do it" to Key VIII as Strength and the eights. You have the strength to follow your chosen spiritual path, to understand your own thoughts and ideas, to maintain your relationships, to advance in your career, to resolve your own financial affairs.

If Key VIII is Justice in your tarot deck you apply these same points to different cards. Select the Pages and Key XI, Strength, and apply the above discussion to these cards instead of the eights. So instead of defining number eight, you'll be defining number eleven for this portion of the course. Please don't consider this incorrect or an inconvenience. It's just different because the author of your tarot deck sees these energies differently than some other authors. When you're ready, proceed to the next section.

# 4

Select the nines, tens, Pages, and Keys IX, X, and XI from your tarot deck. Spread the five nines out in front of you. Review the definitions you've assigned to the five elements and five suits.

The second abstract skill we develop as an adolescent is the concept that other people are watching us and copying us and doing the things we do because we do them. They choose to do the things we do, to have the things we have, to mimic the way we do things. It's flattering, unsettling, and embarrassing. The Hermit and the nines show others the way so they can follow us. The Easy Tarot assigns the key phrase "Be a mentor" and the key concept "Let your light shine" to The Hermit and the nines. Be a mentor to others with your spiritual path, your financial affairs, your career, your relationships, and your thoughts and ideas. You'll need to decide what key word, phrase, or concept you'll assign to number nine.

Set these cards aside and pick up the five tens. The third abstract skill we develop is the concept that what we do to others causes similar things to happen to us. We do receive what we give away. We are treated the way we treat others. What goes around, comes around. In the Easy Tarot we assign the key concept "What you do is done to you" and the key phrase "You receive what you give" to the tens and Key X, the Wheel of Fortune. You receive what you give on your spiritual path, in your career, in your relationships, in your financial affairs, and with your thoughts and ideas. Again, what goes around, comes around. You'll need to decide what key word, phrase, or concept you want to assign to the number ten.

Set these cards aside and pick up the Pages and Key XI. If Key XI is Strength, set aside that key and the Pages as you've already assigned them to inner strength. Instead pick up Key VIII and the four eights and use them for this part of the lesson.

The fourth abstract skill we develop is the concept that the universe is unfailingly just in all things. We're not victims of circumstances. We are the builders of our own circumstances. It's not what happens to us that matters but how we handle what happens to us. Things are exactly as they are because that's the way things are supposed to be. In the Easy Tarot we assign the key concept "Things are exactly the way they're supposed to be" and the key phrase "Unfailingly just" to the Pages and Key XI. Things are exactly as they're supposed to be with your finances, your career, your relationships, your thoughts and ideas, and your spiritual path.

You now have five key words, phrases, or concepts for the five elements. You've assigned one key word, phrase, or concept to the aces through Pages. You've defined fifty-five of your seventy-eight tarot cards and all you have to remember is a total of sixteen key words, phrases, or concepts.

Practice with these fifty-five cards until you firmly implant in your mind the key words, phrases, or concepts you've chosen. When you're ready, proceed to the next section.

## 5

Select Keys XII, XIII, XIV and the Knights, Queens, and Kings from your tarot deck. Place the Knights and Key XII in front of you. Review the meanings you've assigned to the five elements and the five suits.

The fifth abstract concept we develop is the concept that we can change our thinking completely around and still be ourselves. We grow up believing that what we think is right is right, and what we think is wrong is wrong. It's a sign of immaturity that we can't admit we could be wrong. It's a sign of maturity that not only can we admit we might be wrong, but we can change our thinking. In the Easy Tarot we assign the phrase and concept "Change your thinking" to Key XII and the Knights. Change your thinking about your finances, your career, your relationships, your thoughts and ideas (or your belief systems), and your spiritual path. Decide how you want to define the number twelve. Then put these cards aside and spread out the Queens with Key XIII.

The sixth abstract concept we develop is that not only can we change our thinking, we can change our behavior. The old behaviors "die" and new behaviors are "born." We can change who and what we are. In the Easy Tarot we assign the phrase and concept "Change your behavior" to the Queens and Key XIII, Death. You can change your behavior concerning your finances, your career, your relationships, your thoughts and ideas, and your spiritual path. You'll need to decide how you want to define the number thirteen. Then place these cards aside and spread the Kings and Key XIV in front of you.

The seventh and final abstract concept we develop is that we can check into ourselves and verify that what we think, feel, intuit, and do is what we really want to think, feel, intuit, and do. In some mystery schools this is called "Verification." In others it's called "Being prudent" or "Prudence." In the Easy Tarot we assign the key phrase and concept "Verify that this is what you want" to Key XIV and the Kings. Verify that your spiritual path is the one you want, that your career is the one you want, that this relationship is the one you want, that these financial affairs are what you want, and what you think you want is really what you want. You'll need to define the number fourteen the way you want. Then set these cards aside.

At this point in your studies, in addition to whatever practices you're doing with your cards, you might want to consider practicing some one-card readings for a number of questions. Phrase your questions to start with Who, What, When, Where, Which, Why, How, Is or Are, then draw one card to answer your question. (For more information about one-card tarot spreads, see the next chapter in this book.)

You now have five key words, phrases, or concepts for the five elements. You've assigned one key word, phrase, or concept to the aces though the Kings and Keys I through XIV. You've defined seventy of your seventy-eight tarot cards and all you have to remember is a total of nineteen key words, phrases, or concepts. Practice with these seventy cards so you firmly implant in your mind the key words, phrases, or concepts you've chosen. When you're ready, proceed to the next section.

# 6

Select Keys XV through XXI and Key Zero from your tarot deck and lay them out in that sequence. We'll consider them in that order. These final eight cards in our tarot deck describe our spiritual path and only our spiritual path. There are no cards from the Minor Arcana (Pip cards and Court Cards) assigned to these numbers. The first seven numbers are assigned to childhood, the second seven numbers to adolescence, and the last seven cards to adulthood.

Key XV depicts our willing bondage to the physical world of matter. It spans our attraction to matter all the way from complete addiction to the knowledge that our bondage is completely voluntary. In my Gnostic tradition, we believe birth is a decision of our parents and ourselves. We decide to come into this physical reality to learn what we must learn. Some of us get really tied down to the physical reality; we become addicted to one thing or another. Some of us begin to see that this bondage is voluntary. In the Easy Tarot we assign the key words "Bondage" or "Addiction" to the number fifteen. We live in bondage to the world. We're addicted to the world. Either phrase works. Choose one or choose your own definition for the number fifteen.

Key XVI depicts a flash of insight as we awaken to our true being. In a moment we realize we're not our body, we're not our mind, we're not our emotions, we're not our desires, we're not our personality, we're a spiritual being. That moment defines our awakening to the true reality. We realize we're a spiritual being living in a dream world that looks and acts as if it's solid matter. In the Easy Tarot we assign the key words "Awakening" or "Self-realization" to the number sixteen. We awaken to who and what we truly are. We become self-realized. Either phrase works. Choose one or choose your own definition for the number sixteen.

Key XVII depicts a dim light indicating we see the true reality but dimly. We know the truth but only partially. We only have an inkling of the true reality but it's more than we knew before we awakened. We walk under the Star of Hope, in the Starlight of Dark Illumination. The Starlight of Dark Illumination is overcome through contemplation and prayer. The Star of Hope is realized through meditation. In the Easy Tarot we assign the key concept of "Seek more light" or the key word of "Meditate" to the number seventeen. We seek more light (knowledge) on our spiritual path or we meditate to advance on our spiritual path to attain the Star of Hope. Either concept works. Choose one or choose your own definition for the number seventeen.

Key XVIII depicts a deceptive scene where we think we see things clearly but in the moonlight we really don't see things all that clearly some of the time. As the moon waxes and wanes our light shifts from almost darkness to almost light. Moonlight is brighter than starlight and we see more in the starlight than we do in a flash of lightning. Improvement is obvious. In the Easy Tarot we use the key word of "Deception" or the key concept of "Wavering between light and darkness" for Key XVIII. Either works. Choose one or choose your own definition for the number eighteen.

Key XIX depicts the happiness of illumination under the light of the sun. In esoteric circles the human soul is considered to be as bright as the sun. In the Easy Tarot we assign the key word and concept of "Soul consciousness or Christ consciousness or Buddha consciousness" to Key XIX. Any similar concept works. Your spiritual path is attaining soul consciousness in this particular cycle of your growth. Choose one or choose your own definition for the number nineteen.

Key XX depicts a rebirth into a different dimension, a rebirth of our conscious, subconscious, and imaginative minds on a new level. This rebirth is an intermediary step between soul consciousness and God consciousness. In the Easy Tarot we assign the concept of "Rebirth" or "Born again" to Key XX. You've attained a rebirth in your spiritual path.

You're born again into a new you. Either works. Choose one or choose your own definition for the number twenty.

Key XXI depicts the dance of life and is a symbol of cosmic consciousness or God consciousness. We've taken three major steps of self-realization with Key XVI, soul-realization with Key XIX, and now God-realization with Key XXI. In the Easy Tarot we assign the concept of God consciousness or God-realization to Key XXI. Either works. Choose one or choose the definition of your choice for the number twenty-one.

Key Zero depicts us as The Fool who has just made the decision to leave the world of the unmanifest and manifest ourselves in the world of matter. In the Easy Tarot we consider this card as moving from the unmanifest to the manifest and assign that concept to Key Zero. Choose any concept you want to assign to Key Zero and the number zero.

## 7

This completes the short course on the Easy Tarot. My suggestion is to learn these things first, then go back and decide how you want to define the inverted positions for these cards and start using inverted cards as well. Eventually, you may want to add a system for using Tarot Dignities along with inverted cards or in place of them. Thus step-by-step you create your own system for reading tarot cards. That's the best system you could ever use as a tarot reader.

Easy Tarot works very well with just about any tarot spread you want to use. It works particularly well in Dynamic Elemental Spreads, three-card Mind, Body, Spirit or three card Past, Present, Future spreads as well as one-card draws. If you want to experiment with these, they are covered in later chapters of this book.

My suggestion for the beginner is first, to learn how to do one-card draws very well, and move up to larger and larger spreads as you learn. My second suggestion is to learn both the Tree of Life and the Zodiac spreads when you become an accomplished tarot reader. My third suggestion is to use the Celtic Cross spreads only when you can do a good tarot reading. There's nothing worse than a poorly done Celtic Cross. Unfortunately, poorly done Celtic Cross spreads are all too common.

Easy Tarot is compatible with the magical approach to spiritual path working. The material on Tarot and Spirituality in the companion volume *The Tree of Spirit* makes a good introduction to this approach.

Easy Tarot works very well with any definitions you want to use. My fourth suggestion is to change this system by using different words of our choice for the cards of your choice. Recreate this system so it works for you. Be comfortable with the definitions you use. Whatever you decide to change will work. This is a very flexible system and it gives you a lot of latitude to add or subtract what you want to change. My final suggestion is to go for it and do it your way. The best way to continue your studies is to proceed to the next chapter, which will teach you how to do one-card tarot readings.

# CHAPTER 3

# One-card tarot readings

## 1

What?

"What" is a question demanding an answer. "What" questions ask us to tell the other person what they want to know. It's a simple question and all it requires is a simple answer.

One tarot card gives us one simple answer. So all we need to answer any "what" question is one tarot card. Prepare yourself to do a tarot reading. Prepare your tarot deck. Ask yourself: "What's the most important thing for me to accomplish today?" Write this question down in your tarot journal or notebook. Go through your tarot ritual and draw the one card to answer this question. Pick the card. Write down the name of the card and the meaning of this card in your journal. Now answer the question and write out the answer. That's all there is to it.

Here are a few examples from my recent readings:

Q1 – What can I do to find out if he's cheating on me?

A1 – The card drawn for your reading is the Four of Pentacles which means to "organize your finances." You can organize your finances, find out where all the money's going. Then follow the money.

If you can account for all the money, he's probably not cheating on you. If you can't, then you know he's spending it someplace.

Q2 – What can I do to help my son right now?

A2 – The card drawn for your reading is the Page of Cups which means "things are as they should be in all his relationships." The best thing you can do to help your son right now is to recognize he's doing what he wants to be doing and living his life the way he wants to be living it. Realize also that all his relationships are exactly the way he wants them to be. If you do this, that's the best thing you can do to help him right now.

Q3 – What's the best job for me and what's the best place for me to do it?

A3 – The card drawn to answer your first question is the Four of Wands which means "organize your intuitive insights." The best job for you right now is one where you can use your intuition. One where you can organize your intuitive insights to solve problems and help people. The card drawn to answer your second question is the Nine of Wands which means "place of protection." The best place for you to work right now is a place where you feel safe and protected. Any other place would not be good for you.

Q4 – What's the winning lottery numbers today?

A4 – If the tarot cards could give me this answer, you know who the winner would be—me. Let's ask what you need to know about the lottery. The card drawn to answer this question is the Six of Swords which means "let your conscience be your guide in all your thoughts." This card is telling you to let your conscience be your guide whenever you make a decision. That's what you need to know about the lottery.

Q5 – What's the problem with my love life?

A5 – The card drawn for your reading is the Ace of Wands which means "new venture." Evidently you're starting a new venture that's taking up most of your time and energy. That's what's wrong with your love life. You're so busy with your new venture you don't have any time for a relationship. You need to decide what's more important for you right now.

Q6 – What's Shirley doing now that we're apart?

A6 – Tarot cards tell us what we need to know about ourselves. The card drawn for your reading is the Five of Wands which means "conflict between people." This is about you and not Shirley. Evidently you're involved in a conflict you can't seem to resolve. The tarot is telling you to resolve this conflict and get on with your life. It's always hard when relationships fail, but you have to pick up the pieces and pull yourself together. Resolve the conflict and reclaim your life.

You get the idea. The card drawn always answers the question. It tells us what the client needs to do, what would help the client, what would be beneficial and not harmful. The card tells you exactly "What." Your assignment is to ask yourself several "What" questions and answer them with a one-card draw. Write it all down so you have a record. My suggestion is to do one reading each morning and one each evening. Ask any questions you have about any area of your life. Start each question with the word "What."

Here's a little secret: Tarot cards always tell you the truth in all things. If you have any doubts, write it all down and check back later. You'll be amazed to discover that what you didn't believe was true after all.

## 2

Who?

"Who" is a question demanding an answer. "Who" questions ask us to tell the other person about the "whom" they are asking about. It's a simple question and it requires a simple answer. One tarot card gives us one simple answer. So all we need to answer any "who" question is one tarot card.

Prepare yourself to do a tarot reading. Prepare your tarot deck. Ask yourself: "Who's the one person in my life who needs most to hear from me today?" Write this question down in your tarot journal or notebook. Go through your tarot ritual and draw the one card to answer this question. Pick the card. Write down the name of the card and the meaning of this card in your journal. Now answer the question and write out the answer. That's all there is to it.

Here are a few examples from my recent readings:

Q1 – Who stole the money from my wallet?
A1 – The card drawn for your question is the Eight of Pentacles which means "working hard at manual labor." The person who took your money is the person in your life whom you most identify as a hard worker at menial tasks. If you can identify that person, he or she took the money.

Q2 – Who's my soul mate in this lifetime?

A2 – The card drawn for your question is the Page of Cups which means "an inquisitive person looking for romance." You know an inquisitive person looking for romance right now. That person is your soul mate for this lifetime. It just dawned on me that that person might be you. So if you don't know somebody who fits this description, it might be you. If that's the case, then the tarot doesn't have any answer except that you're looking for romance.

Q3 – Who will I marry?

A3 – The card drawn for your question is the Six of Swords which means "passing from rough times into smoother times." The person you're going to marry has been through some rough times but life is getting better. This person was really worried about things until just recently.

Q4 – Who's going to get the job I want?

A4 – The card drawn for your question is the Queen of Wands which means "a person of great energy searching for truth." This person could be you. The person who is going to get the job you seek will be an energetic person looking for the truth about him- or herself and all of reality. This person will be spiritual as well.

Q5 – Who's the best teacher for me right now?

A5 – The card drawn for your question is the Judgement card which means "reborn or rebirth." The person who'll be the best teacher for you right now is the one who is becoming spiritually reborn at this time. You'll know him or her because of their spiritual advancement.

You get the idea. The card drawn always answers the question. It describes an important feature about the person so your client can identify him or her. Sometimes the answer may be a group of people but all the people in that group will be described by the one card drawn.

Your assignment is to ask yourself several "Who" questions and answer them with a one-card draw. Write it all down so you have a record. My suggestion is to do one reading each morning and one each evening. Ask any questions you have about any area of your life. Start each question with the word "Who."

If you have trouble getting comfortable with "who" questions, rephrase the question. As the tarot reader you have the authority to rephrase the questions your clients ask. So rephrase the question so it starts with the word "what." Here's a few examples:

Q1 – Who's my son going to marry?
R1 – What does (name of client) need to know about the person his/ her son's going to marry? or R1—What does (client) need to know about her/his son's marriage?
Q2 – Who'll help me learn to read tarot cards?
R2 – What do I need to know about getting help to read tarot cards? or R2—What does (client) need to know about getting help to read tarot cards?
Q3 – Who needs my help most right now?
R3 – What does (client) need to know about who most needs his/her help?

Rephrasing questions is easy once you give yourself permission to do it. All you have to do is change it from a "who" to a "what" question and focus the question on your client. Make your client the subject of the question rather than a third party.

All "who" questions are third party questions because "who" is not you and it's not your client. Some tarot readers never answer third party questions. As a beginner this is probably a good rule. But it's also a good idea to continue practicing "who" questions.

Here's a little secret: Tarot cards always tell you the truth in all things. If you have any doubts, write it down and check on it later. You'll be amazed to discover what you didn't believe was true after all. Who? It's true.

## 3

When?
   "When" questions demand an answer. "When" questions ask us to identify a time segment in the past or in the future. "When" questions are simple questions requiring a simple answer. One-card tarot readings give simple answers.
   Prepare yourself to do a tarot reading. Prepare your tarot deck. Ask yourself: "When will I learn how to read tarot cards?" Write this question down in your tarot journal or notebook. Go through your tarot

ritual and draw one card to answer this question. The card drawn will explain the last thing you need to accomplish before "when" arrives. Do that thing and that's when. Write down the name and meaning of the card you draw to answer this question. Then do the reading. Write it all down so you'll have this information later when you need it. That's all there is to it. Here are a few examples from my recent readings:

Q4 – When will I ever get married?

A4 – Thank you for requesting this tarot reading. The card drawn to answer your question is the Four of Swords which means "reason it out." As soon as you take the time to think through everything and reason it all out for yourself, you'll get married and not until then. Evidently you've thought about getting married but you haven't taken the time to think through all the things involved in a marriage of two people. When you do, you'll be ready to find the right person and get married. Thank you for asking for this reading. May the answer be a blessing to you. Namaste, Bluejay.

You'll undoubtedly notice that in this example my introduction to the reading has been included, and so has my conclusion, my way of closing the reading and saying good-bye. It's important for you to start to do both an introduction and a closing to your readings.

It's always a good idea to thank your client for asking. It took courage to ask a stranger for help. In thanking the client, my mind is also thanking the universe for bringing this person to me. My thanks is for the confidence the universe has placed in me. My thanks is for the assistance the universe is going to give me to help this person. My thanks is for all the good things the universe does for me.

In closing, my simple prayer is that my reading, done under the supervision of the universe, is going to be a blessing for this client. By sending my positive energy along with this reading, it's my hope my client will find his or her solutions to her or his problems. Silently, my prayer to the universe is thanksgiving for allowing me to be a part of this process.

While you practice this week, and all the following weeks, practice your own greeting and closing. Find something that works for you. Experiment. Try lots of things. Ask other people if what you say sounds like you or some other person. That's always an eye-opener. What do you mean that's not me?

Q5 – When will I ever learn the meaning of all these tarot cards?

A5 – The card drawn for your reading is the Five of Swords which means "taking what doesn't belong to you." In choosing this card, the word "STOP" kept coming to me but it didn't make any sense at the time. The answer to your question is as soon as you stop using the words other people give the tarot cards, you'll learn the meaning of the cards for you. The secret is, tarot cards mean exactly what you say they mean. Nothing more. Nothing less. The words other people use don't belong to you. Your words do.

Q6 – When will the war in Afghanistan be over?

A6 – The card drawn for your reading is the Seven of Cups which means become "receptive to new relationships." As soon as both sides are ready to establish a new relationship, this war will be over and not until then.

Alternatively, I could ask R6—What does (client) need to know about the end of this war?

A6 – The card drawn for your reading is the Ten of Swords which means "destroyed." This war will be over as soon as the enemy is destroyed. That's what you need to know about the end of this war. The question now is: "Who is the enemy?"

"When" questions are answered by a card that identifies the last thing that needs to be done before the event in question will occur. As soon as this last thing is done, the event will happen. One tarot card can always answer "when" questions and describe for you exactly when something will happen. That's when.

Your assignment is to ask yourself several "when" questions and answer them with a one-card draw. Write it all down so you have a record. Share some of these readings with others and compare ideas about answering "when" questions. Do some practice readings for others. Start to use an introduction and a closing with each of your readings. Remember … tarot cards always tell you the truth in all things. Have a great week reading for yourself and others.

4

You should start feeling fairly comfortable with questions starting with "who, what, or when." But if you do experience some unreasonable discomfort, it's OK. Learning pains are common and easily overcome. You always have the option to rephrase the question in order to improve your level of comfort. Always remember that.

Why?

"Why" questions demand an answer. They're simple questions with simple answers and a one-card reading can answer simple questions.

Prepare yourself to do a tarot reading. Prepare your tarot deck. Ask yourself: "Why is this so easy for me after all?" Write this question down in your tarot journal or notebook. Go through your tarot ritual and draw the one card to answer this question. Expect and anticipate the card drawn will be a perfect answer for you. It will be, whether you believe it or not. Write down the name and meaning of the card you drew. Do the reading and write it down too.

Surprised? You shouldn't be. The tarot always tells you the truth. It's your job to discover what that means. By reviewing the questions you ask and the answers you receive, you begin to learn the inner secrets of the tarot. That's why it's so important to write everything down in the beginning. You'll learn more later.

Here's one of my readings from today:

Q1 – Why am I having so much trouble finding my soul mate?
A1 – The card drawn for your reading is the Seven of Pentacles which
     means "procrastination." What this card tells me is you're putting
     off looking for your soul mate. Sitting around and waiting doesn't
     solve anything. You have to work at it. Nothing worthwhile in life
     comes without a price. If you want to find your soul mate, start
     looking. You'll never find him as long as you procrastinate.

This reading seemed a little harsh to me. It seemed like maybe this might be perceived as coming down too hard on her. But, my gut kept telling me to send it off just like it was. You might enjoy hearing her next response. It tickled me: "Boy, are you a lousy fortune teller. I'm not lazy. I work two jobs and I don't have time to go running around looking for anybody." My quick response to her was: "Do you suppose working two jobs might be a form of subconscious procrastination?" She hasn't answered my question yet. But she did hit the nail on the head when she called me a lousy fortune teller. My hope for you is that you are too.

My prayer for all of you is you become a truly wonderful tarot card reader and help lots of people solve their problems; and become a spiritual role model for your clients. Fortune telling is against the law in many areas of our world. Helping people is a lawful and respected profession. Using tarot cards to help people is not fortune telling and using them doesn't make you a fortune teller. What it makes you is a good advisor and respected professional. Don't ever let anybody tell you otherwise.

Your assignment is to continue practicing your introductory remarks and closing comments for your readings. Ask yourself several "why" questions. Offer to answer other people's "why" questions just to gain a little practice. The tarot cards will always tell you why, if you ask. Enjoy your tarot reading and share one or more of them so other tarot readers can enjoy them too.

## 5

Where?

"Where" is a question demanding an answer. "Where" questions ask us to tell the other person where somebody or something is. It's a simple question and all it requires is a simple answer. One card gives us a simple answer. It tells us exactly where the person or thing is. It describes the place where the person or thing is.

Ask yourself any "where" question. Write the question down in your tarot journal or notebook. Go through your tarot ritual and draw one card to answer your question. Write down the name of the card and its meaning in your journal or notebook. Then do the reading. Write out your answer. That's all there is to it.

Here are some examples from my recent readings:

Q1 – Where will I ever find the strength to do what I need to do?
A1 – The card drawn for your reading is the Eight of Swords inverted which means "strong attitude." This card tells me you have the inner strength and the right attitude to resolve this issue now. You don't need to look anywhere else. You have the strength to do it now.
Q2 – Where will I find my social security card?

A2 – The card drawn for your reading is The Fool which means "Get ready to start at the beginning." Evidently you're not going to find your social security card at this time. Starting at the beginning probably means you need to contact the social security administration and discuss your lost card with them.

"Where" questions are not very common except in multiple-card readings. When they do arise, the card drawn will always give the client good advice as to where to look for the answer. But this isn't the only way to answer a "where" question.

Turn the cards one at a time until you come to a court card or a trump. If the card is a court card, the card describes a person who will help the client. If the card is a trump, the message is that the client already knows the answer and the card explains how and why. This technique is useful when the question has to do with finding some intangible like the first example given above.

A variation of this approach is to use all the pip cards drawn in the process to explain the situation in more detail. Assign rooms in the house to the card numbers. Assign areas associated with the client to the card numbers. Then draw the card. Here are a couple of examples to explain how this works:

Q3 – Where did I lose my office keys?
A3 – What are the possibilities? The client helped me make a list of possible locations. The list was assigned to the ranks of the cards in the following manner: 1 – office 2 – automobile 3 – parking lot at work 4 – home driveway 5 – front entry 6 – front room 7 – kitchen 8 – bathroom 9 – bedroom 10 – family room 11 – master bath 12 – office restroom.

We agreed any other rank of card would mean the keys were in somebody else's possession and if that was the case we'd try to identify that person. We also agreed Pentacles would mean the floor, Swords would mean below the knees, Cups would mean between the knees and the belly button, Wands would mean higher than that, and the Major Arcana would mean the keys were inside something else.

Sounds complicated? It really isn't. We had all these things written down and pulled the Page of Cups. The Page represents the number eleven, so the keys were to be found in the master bathroom at about waist level. She searched the bathroom but didn't find the keys. While she was searching the bathroom, she remembered putting the office keys in the console between the front seats of her car.

There's a great secret about the tarot you need to understand. That secret is the tarot always tells the truth. We may not always believe the answers but that's our problem. You might say the keys weren't in the bathroom. They weren't. But when the client searched the bathroom, she remembered where she'd placed the keys and thus "found" them. The tarot will sometimes lead us to the right answer in the most unexpected ways.

Q4 – Where will I find my soul mate?

A4 – We wrote down a list of places where the client might meet his soul mate and assigned numbers to each place. The list looked like this: 1 – the office 2 – church 3 – church social group for singles 4 – the internet singles chat room 5 – singles bar 6 – bimonthly community center dance 7 – a matching service (would need to find one) 8 – while on vacation.

We agreed to divide any number higher than eight by eight and use the remainder. So if The Devil was drawn, we'd divide eight into fifteen once and have a remainder of seven. That would suggest the client join a matching service. The actual card drawn was the Queen of Pentacles. We decided this card might also describe his soul mate as being financially challenged right now. Since eight into thirteen leaves a remainder of five, we decided the singles bar might be the place.

You've got to know this was a very uncomfortable answer for me. Meeting people in bars is not my idea of the best place to find people unless you're looking for a loudmouthed drunk. But that's my hang-up, not his. He seemed pleased with the answer and indicated he thought he knew who this woman might be.

It's easy for me to doubt the cards even after forty-some years of reading them. It's easy for me to let my prejudices get in the way of doing a reading. It's easy for me to think of all kinds of wonderful advice for my clients, to tell them how to live their lives. It's work for me to remember to keep my opinions and prejudices out of my readings all the time. It's work for me to remember the cards will always tell me the truth. It's work for me to remember the cards always give me better answers than my own ideas. As a professional, it's work I must do each and every reading.

This is a good time to ask yourself many who, what, when, where, and why questions for practice. Remember, the difference between a tarot reader and a person who wants to become a tarot reader is nothing more than practice. That's true of all vocations, all hobbies, and all things. The people who practice get better and better. Those who don't, don't.

## 6

Which?

"Which" is a question demanding an answer. "Which" questions ask us to tell the other person which path to follow or which thing to do. Which is a simple question and all it requires is a simple answer. Une card gives us a simple answer. It tells us precisely which person, place, or thing. It describes exactly this person, place, or thing.

Ask yourself any "which" question. Write the question down in your tarot journal or notebook. Go through your tarot ritual and draw one card to answer your question. Write down the name of the card and its meaning in your journal or notebook. Then do the reading. Write out your answer. That's all there is to it. Here's a couple examples from my recent readings:

Q1 – Which job offer should I take?
A1 – The card drawn to answer your question is the Seven of Pentacles which means "wait for results." The better job for you right now is the one which requires you to wait for results. The one where you won't receive instant gratification. (Note: the client knew which job this was and agreed that job was the better choice of the two.)
Q2 – Which should I study first, tarot or astrology?
A2 – The card drawn to answer your question is the inverted Page of Pentacles, which means "balance your attitudes." You need to decide which path would help you balance your attitudes. This suggests you might want to study first the one which concerns you the most. (Note: The client indicated having more concerns about reading tarot cards because her family was fundamentalist Pentacostal.)
Q3 – Which system should I use? (A or B?)
A3 – The card drawn to answer your question is The Fool which means "get ready to begin." This would lead me to believe the system

which would be a completely new system for you is the better of the two systems. (The client knew which one that was.)

This brings up an interesting issue all tarot readers need to face some time. What if the answer didn't make any sense to the client? What if both systems were going to be completely new? Or what if neither system was newer than the other?

Some tarot readers approach this issue by telling the client to think about the answer, to give it some time so the answer makes sense. They tell the client to write the question and answer down (this is a good idea anyway) and wait for the answer to make sense.

Other tarot readers approach this issue by drawing another card to further explain the situation, to add more information to the answer. The second card doesn't change the first answer, it clarifies the answer and makes it easier to understand.

A few tarot readers scrap the first reading as an error and do another reading altogether. This is my least favorite solution because it sends the message to my subconscious mind that it made a mistake. It's like blaming somebody else for my problem. My problem is neither my client nor my subconscious mind. My problem is that I don't understand the answer. To me, that's my problem and not the result of an error made by my subconscious mind.

A few tarot readers draw another card to help them understand the answer better. The card tells the reader something to help interpret the first card drawn. This card doesn't clarify the answer for the client, it helps the reader understand the answer better.

How you choose to resolve this issue is up to you. My approach is to use my intuition to guide me. It will often tell me to draw another card for the client or for myself. Occasionally, my intuition says to wait and the answer will become clear. It's been a long, long time since I scrapped a reading because it didn't make sense to me or my client at the time. As a matter of fact, when I stopped scrapping readings because I didn't understand them, my readings started getting a lot better. Maybe my subconscious mind was sending me a message after all.

Q4 – Which food is causing my son's allergy?

A4 – The card drawn for your reading is the Ace of Wands which means new energy or new enterprise. Evidently your son has tried a new food to increase his energy and this is causing him a problem.

My suggestion to you is to remove this food item from his diet and later reintroduce it. Check out the results to see if it really is a food allergy. My other suggestion is to consult your family physician or health provider regarding his possible allergy to certain foods.

This raises another major issue all tarot readers need to address. The client is asking for a third party reading for information about his or her son. That means you, as a tarot reader, need to tune in to his or her son through the client. It can be done, but not easily. My suggestion for all neophyte tarot readers is to avoid doing third party tarot readings until you're confident you can do them. Careful. Your imagination and ego will try to convince you you're ready before you really are. Make sure.

My recommendation is that you don't do readings like the example just given. Rather, my suggestion is to rephrase the question so it's about your client. Then do the reading. Should you decide not to do third party readings, you need to learn how to rephrase the client's question into a question about the client. Here's how:

Q4 – Which food is causing my son's food allergy?
R4 – What does (client) need to know about his/her son's food allergies?

The rephrased question is about the client and not the client's son. It's much easier to read for your client than for somebody else.

A4 – The card drawn for your reading is The Hierophant which means "intuition." This suggests that you trust your intuition in this matter and be guided thereby.

This particular reading was done for another tarot reader. The rephrased question was answered first and the client acknowledged her intuition had already identified the problem food. The actual question was then answered as an example of how a third party reading might be done. The client stated that this is the same answer she had received intuitively already.

It takes lots of practice to be able to tune through your client to another person. My recommendation is to learn to tune in to your client and become a good tarot reader first. Then try tuning through your client to another person. Learn to rephrase your questions. Practice doing as many tarot readings as you can.

# 7

How?

"How" is a question demanding an answer. "How" questions ask us to tell the other person how to do something. How is a simple question and all it requires is a simple answer. One card gives us a simple answer. It tells us exactly how something can be done.

Ask yourself any "how" question. Write the question down in your tarot journal or notebook. Go through your tarot ritual and draw one card to answer your question. Write down the name of the card and its meaning in your journal or notebook. Then do the reading. Write out your answer. That's all there is to it. Here are a couple examples from my recent readings:

Q1 – How can I learn to read tarot cards?
A1 – The card drawn for your reading is the inverted Moon which means "You have a problem deceiving yourself." My feeling is you've convinced yourself the experts are right and you're wrong. Therefore you're trying to learn the cards by memorizing how some expert does it. If this is what you're doing, you're deceiving yourself. You'll never become a carbon copy of that expert. But you can become yourself and you can learn to read tarot cards by using your own definitions for each card.

You may think this reading is made up, but it isn't. It's an actual reading for a beginning student who decided to build her own system for reading tarot cards. She's now doing a bang-up job on the FreeTarot network doing free one-card readings for the public. Her system works for her and she gives quite accurate readings.

Your system will work for you. The more you try to memorize somebody else's system, the harder it'll be for you to learn to read tarot cards and the longer it'll take you. The more you rely on your own life experiences, your own feelings about what each card should mean for you, the easier it is. The faster you learn. The better reader you become. The better your readings become. The happier your clients will be. Your system will work for you.

Q2 – How can terrorists justify blowing up the Twin Towers?
R2 – What does (client) need to know about handling issues involving terrorist activities?

A2 – The card drawn for your reading is the Wheel of Fortune which means "what goes round, comes round." You need to be aware what the terrorists are doing to others will also happen to them but to a greater degree. Their pain will be greater because they caused so much pain for others. You have no control over what the terrorists might do. You do have control over how you react to their terror.

This is an example of rephrasing which we have already considered. The question was rephrased into terms about the client rather than the terrorists. Advanced tarot readers could answer the original question, but beginners are well advised to rephrase such questions. Here's how the original question might have been answered:

Q2 – How can terrorists justify blowing up the Twin Towers?
A2 – The card drawn for your reading is the inverted Hanged Man which means they "have a problem with changing their think-ing." Obviously the terrorists see life differently than we do and they have a problem understanding us. They can't reason things through clearly because their emotions are running wild. So they ignore the greater truth of their actions because they can't change the way they think about us.

That reading wasn't given until just now. My original answer was the one given using the rephrased question. This is an example of a third party reading where the reader attempts to tune directly into the third party without going through the client. It can be done, with practice. There's that practice word again. It must be important.

Q3 – How can I find a good meaning for the Four of Wands?
A3 – The card drawn for your readings is The Fool which means "pre-pare for a new beginning." This indicates to me you've exhausted all the possibilities you've raised and didn't find anything that worked for you. The Fool suggests trying something new. If you don't use astrology, maybe you might find something there to help you. If you don't use numerology, maybe you'll find something there to help you. Astrologically, the Four of Wands is normally associated with Jupiter the planet of good fortune, education, philosophy, religion, spirituality, good deeds and good things.

Numerologically, the number four refers to bringing things back into balance, to squaring them, bringing order to them. If any of these things strikes a chord with you, you're on the right track. Please let me know if you need further assistance or if this information was helpful.

Do you see it? There's my doubt coming back into my reading. Unfortunately the email was already gone before this came to my attention. My doubt made me ask the client if she needed further assistance to contact me. My doubt made me ask her to let me know if this was helpful. My doubt made me say if any of these things strike a chord she's on the right track. Keeping my doubt out of my readings is work and sometimes we all get lazy.

That's not an excuse. It's an acknowledgement that my readings are not perfect. Readings never are. What they are is helpful, eye-opening, inspirational, and lots of other things but they're never absolutely perfect. Close but not perfect. Informational but not perfect. Good but not perfect. All I need is more practice.

If you're not laughing, you're taking this too seriously. We say practice makes perfect. What it does is make us very good. In this lifetime very few people reach perfection and do perfect things. Most of us are prone to error. We make mistakes. We try. We all need more practice. The very best tarot readers known to me are still practicing. Most of them every day. They practice by doing readings for themselves and others. They even get paid for practicing! So can you if you practice your tarot readings and continue to become better and better.

Q4 – How can I find peace?
A4 – The card drawn for your reading is The Magician which means "pay attention to your spiritual path." The Magician tells me you've gotten away from your spiritual practices. You've become too involved in life's problems. It's time to pay attention to your spirituality if you want to find peace.

How true that answer rings for me right now in my life too. That often happens. Sometimes when we give readings for other people, we get answers that make sense in our lives right then too. Isn't it interesting that the universe would send us a client with the same problem we have? It happens all the time, so don't be surprised when your readings seem to apply to you. They might. But they also apply to your client. After all, the reading was done for your client. Not you. Your client and you, yes, but never just for you. It's your client's reading. If it also applies to you that's a bonus. Just don't forget that the client asked the question and you have the answer.

This short lesson completes our investigation into the Seven Rays of Discernment, the seven questions of journalism, and the Seven Spiritual Questions. They are: what, when, where, which, who, why, and how. Almost eighty percent of the questions you'll receive will be in this form. Or they can be rephrased into this form. The other twenty percent is our topic for the next lesson.

## 8

Is? Are? Will? Am?

These kinds of questions beg for a yes or no answer. Using one card we can answer these kinds of questions using any one of several techniques.

You can decide upright cards mean "yes" and inverted cards mean "no." This requires you to shuffle your cards in such a manner that some cards remain upright and others are inverted. This can be done by cutting the deck into two halves and inverting one pile with respect to the other. Then shuffle. Repeat.

Prepare the deck and yourself to do a reading. Use your normal ritual. Draw one card to answer the question. If this card is upright, the answer is yes. If not, the answer is no. The meaning of the card itself can be used to explain the answer in a little more detail.

Q1 – Is Shawn going to ask me to marry him?
A1 – The card drawn for your reading is the inverted Seven of Pentacles which means "procrastination." It appears Shawn isn't going to ask you to marry him at this time. He's procrastinating. You need to decide if you're willing to wait, want to push him out of his procrastination, or move on. Good luck.

Tarot gives great answers for us but has a hard time answering questions for others. In answer to the rephrased question "What does (client) need to know about her relationship with Shawn?" the card drawn was the Three of Cups which means "romantic love and friendship." Evidently you've found a man worth having in your life. The two of you appear to be right for each other. If he's open to discussing these issues, you might want to raise the possibility of sharing the rest of your lives together. Good luck.

The first reading is the actual reading given to the client. The second is an example of how a beginner might handle the same question by rephrasing it. It's interesting to me how similar these readings turned out to be. The more expertise you have as a tarot reader the more you can expect this to be so. Does that suggest practice?

Q2 – Am I kidding myself about becoming a tarot reader?

A2 – The card drawn for your reading is The Magician which means "pay attention to your spiritual life." Yes, it appears you're kidding yourself about becoming a tarot reader right now. You have a higher priority right now and that's to pay attention to your spiritual path. Once you've addressed this issue you may find tarot to be a useful tool for helping you improve your spirituality. Good luck.

Here's an example of how an upright card gave a negative response in a positive manner. My guess is that this reader will incorporate tarot into her spiritual work and eventually become a very good tarot reader. Right now her first priority is her spiritual path. She agreed.

Q3 – Would you suggest we move from our present home?

Here's a puzzle you need to figure out for yourself. The client is asking me, the reader, to make a decision for the client. That's not my responsibility. Here's my response:

A3 – The card drawn for your reading "What does (client) need to know moving from his present home?" is the inverted Strength card which means "you have a problem finding the strength within yourself to solve your problems." This suggests it doesn't matter where you live. What's important is for you to know you have the inner strength to handle all the obstacles in your life. You have this inner strength to solve your own problems and you can use this strength any time you want. That's what's important for you to know right now.

Making decisions for others is not my style. It always got me in trouble, every time. Avoiding trouble is one of my goals, so making decisions for others is not a good thing for me to do. When clients ask me to make decisions for them, it's time for me to rephrase their question.

There are a few variations of the Is? Are? Will? Am? questions you also need to learn how to handle. These are the Could? Would? Can? Should? questions which also beg for a yes or no answer. They also beg for you to make a decision for the client.

Q4 – Should I marry Harry?
A4 – No, because the cards say no.

Right. That's not a decision I'm comfortable making. No matter what answer the cards give me, that answer is going to be wrong some time in the client's life. If the card is upright and my answer is yes and the marriage turns our badly, who's to blame? The client may blame me. The client's lawyer may blame me. The judge may blame me. Those options don't appeal to me. If the marriage turns out great will the client credit me then? What if the card is inverted and the answer is no. The client either gets married anyway or calls the whole thing off. The client's fiancé may blame me. The fiancé's attorney may blame me. The judge may blame me. These options don't appeal to me either. Besides, the client's life may turn out badly and the client may blame me. So might the client's attorney or the judge. That's not good for me either.

Q5 – Am I pregnant?
Q6 – Is my husband sleeping with my boyfriend's wife?
Q7 – Are my children doing drugs?

Do you see a pattern here that might be dangerous to your financial well-being? Do you see any option for rephrasing these questions into "What does (client) need to know about ...?" If you do, then you've found a safe way to handle these kinds of questions. If not, you might want to study how to rephrase questions to focus on the client.

The truth is that these questions can be answered using tarot cards. The truth is that the answers may not be well received. The truth is that the client can make some changes in his or her life and change the answer at some future date. The truth is that these kinds of questions are best avoided by beginning tarot readers. The best way to avoid them is to rephrase them. It's fun to ask a friend these kinds of questions so the friend can practice rephrasing the questions. It's also fun fielding some of these kinds of questions and rephrasing them. Practice can be fun. Enjoy it.

## 9

Is? Are? Will? Am? Do? Does?

There are other ways of answering these types of questions besides using inverted cards for "no" and upright cards for "yes." One way is to use numerology. Here all the odd numbers mean "no" and all the even numbers mean "yes." Pages and Queens are considered odd (11 and 13) while Knights and Kings are considered even (12 and 14). Using that system gives the following answers for these made-up questions:

Q1 – Does my car need new tires?
A1 – The card drawn for this reading is the Two of Swords which means yes, your car needs new tires. You might want to double-check this with a tire expert in your local community.
Q2 – Is my cancer returning?
A2 – The card drawn to answer the question: "What does (client) need to know about cancer and her health is the Three of Pentacles inverted. This card indicates that your health is improving. Your question about cancer can only be answered by a qualified health care practitioner. My suggestion is that you contact your health care provider right away to discuss this issue.

Notice how this question was rephrased. Any answer containing "yes" or "no" could be construed as practicing medicine without a license. That's not a good place to go unless you happen to be a licensed health care provider who can legally diagnose cancer under the law. "Yes, you have cancer" is a diagnosis. "No, your cancer is not returning" is also a diagnosis. There's no easy way to answer such questions with either a "yes" or a "no."

Some tarot readers will actually answer questions of this type with a "yes" or a "no." Whether they're right or wrong in their diagnosis really doesn't matter. What matters is whether the authorities hear about that particular tarot reading or not. Charges may be filed for practicing medicine without a license or for fortune telling. Neither charge does the tarot reader any good.

Charges may not be filed, but an investigation into the tarot reader's activities may be initiated. Such an investigation will eventually cause the reader trouble. Why? Because we all tend to repeat doing the same kinds of things we've done before. Such readers seldom diagnose disease only once in their lifetime. Doing such a diagnosis while being investigated is probably not in the reader's best interest.

Alternatively, the authorities may never hear anything because the reader was right. This means the reader was right for the rest of the client's life. Why? If things ever change, and things usually do change, the reading is now false. If and when this happens, the tarot reader's words may come back to haunt him or her. Some questions are better answered after they're rephrased.

Q3 – Is my financial problem ever going to get better?
A3 – The card drawn for your reading: "What do I need to know about my financial situation?" is the Queen of Swords which means that you need to "change your behavior." You need to change your behavior with money and financial affairs before things can improve. Evidently you're spending more than your income and tarot cards can't solve that problem for you. My advice is for you to seek competent financial advice from a financial expert. These people are trained to help you solve your financial problems. Financial advisors are listed in the Yellow Pages. Your family, friends, minister, banker, or attorney may know a financial advisor who can help you. Good luck.

Again the question was rephrased and my personal code of ethics was enforced. The original question was not answered, but the client received useful information. This raises another question: "Is it right to charge a fee for such advice?" That's a question you'll need to answer for yourself. The truth is that you're entitled to a fee anytime you do a reading for a client. The truth is that you may not feel this fee was earned. The truth is that if you give the client valuable information, that's worth a fee. Information has value and you're entitled to a fee when you share valuable information. My personal approach is to give such advice freely and not accept any fee for doing so. But, that's just my opinion.

Here again, some tarot readers do give financial advice. In my opinion they're flirting with the law and may not like the end result. When you give advice such as this without a license to do so, you're going to anger the people who do have a license to give such advice. Angry people do angry things. Judges and lawyers tend to favor persons with the proper license. When your advice is good the chances are nobody will do anything against you. However, if your advice turns sour, you may be in a bad situation.

The problem is time. Advice that's really great for today may be wrong tomorrow. Things change but the words you spoke yesterday do not change. People tend to forget that the situation changes if they can blame somebody else for their problems. This is the way tarot readers get labeled as charlatans. Truth is that police, attorneys, and judges dislike charlatans. So does the public.

Whatever you do, be professional. You cannot be the best you can be by giving advice in these situations. If the question begs for medical, financial, or legal advice, your best approach is to refer your client to the proper experts. If the question begs for any answer you consider to be unethical in any way, your best approach is to refer this client to the proper experts. If the question makes your intuition scream: "Don't answer that," then don't. Refer your client to an expert legally qualified to answer his or her question. That's my advice.

Q4 – Will I get pregnant this month?
Q5 – Is my husband cheating on me?
Q6 – Will my brother go to Hell for killing that man?
Q7 – Is this the best stock for my retirement?
Q8 – Are my husband and I going to lose our home?
Q9 – Am I investing in the right stocks to make money?

Decide how you're going to answer these questions. Be prepared to refer your clients to attorneys, doctors, counselors, ministers, and advisors of all kinds. Be prepared to rephrase your clients' questions and answer the rephrased question. Be professional in all you do. That's my advice.

You can use the elements instead of numbers to decide whether the answer is "yes" or "no." For example, the masculine elements of Fire and Air could mean "yes" while the feminine elements of Water and Earth could mean "no." Using this system you need to decide how to handle the Major Arcana. One way is to always make them neutral, meaning there's no answer yet. Another way is to consider the Keys I through XIV as positive or "yes" and the other Keys as "no." My favorite way of handling the Major Arcana using this approach is to have them mean both "yes" and "no." The meaning of the card can then be used to explain the situation. Here's a couple of examples using that approach:

Q10 – Am I going to graduate from college?

A10 – The card drawn for your reading is The Fool which means "before the beginning." This card tells me the answer is both yes and no. Yes, you will graduate from college if you decide that's what you really want to do. No, you won't graduate from college if that's what you decide instead. You're at the place before the beginning. To go anywhere you need to make the decision if you want to finish college or not.

Q11 – Is my ex-husband really gay?

A11 – The card drawn for this reading is the Four of Cups which indicates the answer is no in this system. But that's leading you astray. The card drawn to answer the question: "What does (client) need to know about her ex-husband's sexuality" is the Four of Cups which means "organize your relationships." This suggests to me that you need to decide what your ex-husband's sexuality has to do with you. You need to decide what impact this really has on you and how important it is to you.

Rephrase this kind of question. It doesn't matter how you answer the original question, you'll be wrong. If her ex-husband is gay and you say he is, nothing may happen. Then again, he may go straight sometime in the future and make you out a liar. If her ex-husband is gay and you say he isn't, you made a mistake and mistakes can cause you problems. Those problems will probably be quite small compared to saying her ex-husband is gay when he really isn't. If her ex-husband isn't gay and you say he isn't, nothing may happen. However, he may decide at some future date he is gay and that makes you out a liar again. How can you win?

The real question isn't whether her ex-husband is gay or not. The real question is what she's going to do about it, how she's going to react, how she's going to behave, how it'll make her feel. The real question is about the client and not about her ex-husband. My suggestion is to answer the real question and forget about third parties as much as you can, especially as a beginning reader.

Q12 – Am I going to get a raise in my present employment?

A12 – The card drawn for your reading is the Page of Swords which means yes, you will. The Page suggests bringing new ideas to your job will help you get a raise. This is the good news. The bad news is the financial situation with your employer may change and you may not get that raise. But if things don't change, you will receive a raise at work. My suggestion is don't spend that money until you get it.

The secret to success in all things is practice.

## 10

You've already learned how to handle most of the questions you'll be asked by using the seven basic questions and yes/no questions. Many of these same questions can be answered using an elemental spread. The five elements are Earth, Water, Air, Fire, and Spirit. These can yield no less than ten basic questions by defining each element two different ways. Here are some possibilities:

Earth:  body, health, financial affairs
Water:  relationships, friendships, emotions
  Air:  mind, thoughts and ideas, attitudes
 Fire:  energy, career, intuition
Spirit:  spirituality, spiritual path, spiritual goals, spiritual obstacles

One card can describe any one of these things. Choose several things from this list and you have several one-card readings. Add to this list the things you decide the elements will mean for you. Delete those things you don't want the elements to represent. Make up your own list of possibilities for doing one-card elemental readings. Then practice doing one-card elemental readings.

Elemental readings are my choice for answering general questions about life, relationships, jobs, finances, health, and other general topics.

By intuitively tuning in to your client you decide which of the categories you'll use and how many of them. Here's a couple examples from my readings:

Q1 – Tell me about my job situation.

Note: By tuning in to the client, the categories selected for this reading were finances, health, and career. This could be called an Earth-Earth-Fire spread or a Money-Body-Career spread. My approach is not to name the spread but to name the parts of the spread. So one card was drawn for each of the one-card readings on finances, health, and career. Then three separate one-card readings were done.

A1 – The cards drawn for your reading are:
      Finances – The Tower inverted
      Health – Two of Cups
      Career – The World

You have a problem not knowing the financial situation in your present job. This is a major problem for you and suggests you may be looking for another situation. Intuitively your health became an issue for this reading. The message of the Two of Cups is your health is friendly to your career and is not being adversely affected by it. However, if health is a concern for you, my suggestion is to contact your health provider and get some answers. Put your mind at ease.

The final card tells me you've already decided to end your present situation and you're actively looking for a new position. It's a wise decision to find your new position while you're still employed. This card also tells me you will find exactly what you're looking for.

There are three things that you as a student need to know about this reading. First, the last statement was made because two trumps appeared in a three-card reading and that's very positive for the client in my system. Second, each one of these three readings stands alone as a one-card tarot reading. Third, this is not your standard Mind-Body-Spirit spread. Both the M-B-S spread and my spread are examples of elemental spreads.

Q2 – Give me a general reading.
A2 – The cards drawn for your reading are:

Finances – The Moon
Relationships – Two of Swords
Spiritual – Knight of Swords

The cards indicate that you're caught up in your own thoughts and ideas (Swords) and may be applying too much mental activity to your relationships both physical and spiritual. The Two of Swords advises you to remember past ideas that you've had regarding relationships. Follow those ideas forward in time to the final result in the relationship. Then use this knowledge to forge new relationships. Intuitively this card is telling me you need to learn from past mistakes.

The Knight of Swords indicates you have some wrong ideas about spirituality and what a spiritually based life looks like. True spirituality operates for the good of all. It is not selfish. It's not about you. It's about the people in your life. Change your ideas about spirituality and you change the results you've been achieving in the past.

This brings us to the Moon which tells us you've been kidding yourself about your financial situation. My guess is this is all tied up with the relationships in your life and your spiritual outlook on life. Money can be both a blessing and a curse. If you use it for selfish means or to gain control over others, money is a curse in your life. If you use it for the benefit of others and to free yourself, money is a blessing. You get to decide how you'll handle your financial affairs. The Moon advises you to stop deluding yourself about money and make it part of your spirituality, part of your spiritual path.

Note: Again this is three separate one-card readings. The power of the trump weighed heavily on the other two readings. That points up both a benefit of larger readings and a problem interpreting larger readings. The beginner is not prepared to interpret the nuances of a three-card tarot reading. Those who stumble ahead without first mastering one-card readings, rarely succeed.

Having been in the position to evaluate not hundreds, but thousands of tarot readers, this truth emerges above all others: It doesn't matter how long you've been reading tarot cards. What matters is how well you read them. It's been my pleasure to watch an eighteen year old do marvelous tarot readings after studying for less than one year. This young person is a master of one-card tarot readings and does superb readings with the Tree of Life and the Celtic Cross spreads.

It's also been my unfortunate duty to inform a person with eighteen years' experience doing tarot readings that he/she did not qualify as a Certified Professional Tarot Reader. Later it came to my attention that two other evaluators had previously given this person the same news. The reader never learned to use any other spread except the Celtic Cross. Her/his readings with this spread are disjointed, confusing, and almost incomprehensible. Nothing makes sense, even to the reader. Rarely does anybody ever ask her/him for another reading. This reader is always looking for new clients and not building positive reader-client relationships. Professional tarot readers will tell you the secret to making money as a professional tarot reader is repeat customers. Repeat customers are the single most important thing you need as a professional tarot reader.

My suggestion to this person was to learn how to do one-card tarot readings. The Celtic Cross is really nothing more than a three-card Past-Present-Future spread, a one-card spread about the most important issue in the client's life, a three-card Support-Situation-Obstacles spread, and four one-card spreads up the side with the last four cards. To my surprise, she/he joined the Free Tarot Network, signed up for the Introduction to Tarot course and started working from the beginning. Within sixty days this person was enrolled in the Intermediate Tarot course and doing three-card readings on the Free Reading Network. It pleases me greatly to tell you today this individual is not only a professional tarot reader but a good tarot teacher and mentor who attained the rank of Certified Tarot Instructor in eighteen months.

The secret is not how long you've been reading the cards but how well you read them. In my opinion, those tarot readers who learn how to do excellent one-card tarot readings have a very real advantage over those who don't. They learn more quickly. They learn how to do better tarot readings. They become certified faster and higher. They really are better tarot readers. They understand their tarot cards better and they give better readings. Their clients come back for more.

Practice one-card tarot readings until you master them. Practice doing as many different one-card elemental spreads for yourself and others. Learn how to use the power of the spread to obtain great answers. Relate the meaning of the card to the element of the card. Then relate this to the element you chose for the spread. That's all there is to it.

*11*

Pick a subject, any subject. Decide which element this is and you've just created a one-card elemental spread. Pick another subject, and another. Decide which elements these are and you've just created a three-card elemental spread. Pick as many subjects as you want and create elemental spreads of any size. Then practice doing one-card readings with as many of these as you decide.

The time to start tying them together into a comprehensive reading is later. Right now concentrate on doing great one-card tarot readings. You'll be absolutely amazed at how accurate your readings can become. You'll be invigorated by the power of one-card readings.

In one of my classes several students challenged me to do a ten minute, one-card tarot reading. They thought the reading could be covered in a couple of minutes and more cards would be needed to get a good answer. One student picked the subject. My choice was to do an elemental spread of one card. The reading kept them all spellbound for almost twenty minutes. That one card gave them more information than they thought possible. Today most of them can do the same thing.

Once you know your cards and understand one-card readings, you can talk for a long time about any one card for any one reading. That's a gift. It's also a curse.

Clients generally want simple and quick answers, especially if they're paying by the minute. You need to learn all you can about each of the tarot cards. You also need to learn how to give precise answers to questions quickly and efficiently. How can you do this? Are you ready for this?

Practice.

The more you practice the better you become. The more you practice the quicker you learn. The more you practice the easier it is for you to do tarot readings using spreads of any size, any time, any place. Better tarot readers who know more about their cards and give better readings make more money than other tarot readers. You can bank on that whether you decide to become a full-time professional tarot reader or a part-time one.

There's one more type of spread you need to consider: temporal spreads. "Temporal" is a fancy word meaning time. So, these are spreads concerning time. Time in the past or in the future can be divided into segments of any length. Time in the present is now and only now. Therefore, temporal spreads can have as many cards in the past and in the future as you want, but the present is best served by just one card.

One of my favorite time spreads is to look at three, six, and twelve months ago as well as three, six, and twelve months into the future. The present situation is represented by one card. That makes an intense seven-card, in-depth reading on any subject the client wants to discuss. It's so flexible it can be used for a fifteen minute reading or a one hour reading. If this looks like a series of one-card spreads to you, that's a very good sign you're learning how to do professional quality tarot readings. You're not there yet, but you're learning. You can make it if you do three things: 1) practice, 2) practice, and 3) practice.

You're at least smiling, right?

One-card time spreads can really be quite illuminating. All "when" questions are based on time. Some "what" questions relate to time. Here are some sample questions asking for an answer based on time:

Q1 – What's the most important thing for me to learn this month?
Q2 – What changed three months ago to get me where I am?
Q3 – When will my financial situation start to change?
Q4 – Is this month or next a better time to start my business?
Q5 – What in a previous lifetime can help me learn this lesson?

Yes, time readings can be used to explore past lifetimes as well as this one. You can probe your early childhood and even your experiences in the womb. Time is eternal so you have no limit as to what past or future time you can explore.

One caution. As you explore these things make very certain you don't let your imagination get carried away. Write everything down and keep a full and complete record. Invite and expect intuitive insights but don't over-think anything. With practice you'll become very competent working with time in your tarot readings.

You can also use time spreads to identify the lesson being learned right now. Here's a recent reading to illustrate that point. The client identified three turning points in his life and wondered which one of them was impacting his present financial difficulties the most. The cards drawn for his reading were:

Turning Point 1:  Key 13, Death
Turning Point 2:  Five of Swords
Turning Point 3:  Seven of Cups

It's immediately obvious to me the first turning point is the one having the most impact on his present financial difficulties. The deceit seen in the Five of Swords and the illusion of truth in the Seven of Cups are minor occurrences in life compared to the changes brought about by a trump card. A major change in behavior is called for by Death.

Turning point spreads are more difficult if no trump card appears in the reading. That's why some tarot readers keep adding cards to the spread until a trump appears. Let's say the seventh card was the first trump. The first three cards were distributed to Turning Points 1-2-3. The second three cards were also distributed to TP 1-2-3. The seventh card would go on the first stack and no more cards are pulled for this reading. Then you need to analyze the cards drawn and the turning points to make a decision.

Turning point readings are also more complicated if more than one trump card appears in the spread. You can use the number of the trump if you like. The higher numbered trump card is the one most readers use as being the stronger of the two. You can also compare the trumps to the turning points to see which has more implications on the client's present financial situation. You also have the option of drawing more cards to clarify the situation.

Another way to handle turning point readings is to draw one card and see which of the turning points this card is most closely aligned with. The single card will resonate with one of the turning points more than the others. You've just identified the critical turning point for this client's question.

Any time you have several options, you can draw one card to identify which option is the preferred solution. This process is similar to how you'd handle "which" questions. Some such questions actually are "which" questions. They can also be "when" questions.

Take a turning point and ask when this turning point will be fully resolved. Or ask when the outcome will be realized. Or ask when this turning point will be repeated. Such questions actually are "when" questions. As we learned earlier, they can also be "what" questions.

The three-card temporal spread of Past-Present-Future is probably the most commonly used three-card tarot spread. It's really three one-card readings tied together by a common spread. Looking at all time spreads in this manner will make these spreads easier to do. Try a few temporal spreads before you proceed.

## 12

Some professional tarot readers like to pull an "outcome" card as the final card for any reading. An outcome card is a one-card tarot reading addressing the final result. You can add an outcome card to any spread.

Some tarot readers like to have a card dedicated to "obstacles" which identifies problems that need to be resolved. Obstacles can also be issues or concerns. No matter what you call them, they're just another example of a one-card tarot reading. You can add an obstacle card to any spread.

Some tarot readers like to have a card dedicated to "assistance" which identifies what kind of assistance you can expect from others or from the universe. You probably already guessed this is another example of a one card reading which can be added to any spread. As a tarot reader you get to choose what spreads you'll use. You get to choose what names you'll give to the positions within the spread. You get to choose how you're going to do the reading. In short, you get to decide:

1. What questions you answer
2. What deck you use
3. How you'll define each card
4. If you use inverted cards
5. If you use dignities
6. How you'll define the elements
7. Which elements you assign to which suits
8. How you'll care for your deck
9. How you'll shuffle the cards
10. How you select the cards
11. Which tarot spreads you'll use
12. What the positions within the spread mean
13. When to rephrase a question
14. How you interpret the reading
15. And a whole lot of other things

Practice. Practice. Practice. That's my advice.

# CHAPTER 4

# Dynamic Elemental Spreads

*1*

The first set of spreads we'll consider in this chapter are what I call the Dynamic Elemental Spreads. We'll begin by defining each of the five elements. Then we'll assign each element to one of the five tarot suits. Then we'll define the Dynamic Elemental Spreads and start reading.

It'll really help if you've already defined each of the seventy-eight tarot cards with the meanings and interpretations you want to use. The better you know and understand your cards, the easier these spreads will be to use. At the very least, you will need to know one key word, phrase, or concept for each card. It's even better if you have both the upright and reversed meanings for each card well defined. We'll start by reviewing the standard meanings of the elements here. If you have a different set of meanings you use for the elements, of course, use those instead.

**Fire**: Fire is usually defined as "will" or the "will to do something." Fire is the driving force behind everything we do. It's the drive we have to accomplish anything, the desire we have to do anything. Fire is there-fore usually considered to be will, willpower, determination, intention, perseverance, drive, eagerness, zeal, zealousness, avidness, enthusiasm, desire, fortitude, single-mindedness, passion, gusto, inspiration, insight, intuition, career, work, and occupation.

**Water:** Water is usually defined as "relationships" or "emotions." Water is the receptive power that enables us to interact with our environment and each other. It's the acceptance we have of things the way they are and the way we'd like them to be. Water is therefore usually considered to be relationships, friendship, amity, love, emotions, fondness, liking, warmth, affection, devotion, tenderness, romance, adoration, adulation, attachment, admiration, addiction, craving, and feelings of hopelessness, helplessness, and unworthiness.

**Air:** Air is usually defined as "thought" or "ideas." Air is the ability to think both consciously and subconsciously. Some people even include "unconsciously." It's the basis for knowing, understanding, and communicating. Air is therefore usually considered to be thought, cogitation, ideas, concepts, conception, perception, contemplation, meditation, hope, expectations, planning, order, organized, pondering, planning, goal-setting, understanding, wisdom, opinion, orientation, disposition, reaction, psychological, attitude, and demeanor.

**Earth:** Earth is usually defined as "possessions" or "things." Earth is the material world and everything in it. It's the physical reality in which we live. Earth is therefore usually considered to be things, possessions, objects, articles, utensils, property, belongings, assets, worldly goods, the physical body, health, condition, fitness, disease, illness, constitution, vigor, money, currency, cash, or wealth. Some authors also consider Earth to be personality, nature, temperament, grooming, clothing, and things we wear to express our personality.

**Spirit:** Spirit is usually defined as our "spirituality" or our "spiritual path." Spirit is the essence of life within us that's expressed as our individuality. It's also the spiritual path we're traveling to become a better person than we are now. Spirit is spiritual, spirituality, sacred space, psychic, nonmaterial, our inner being, and our awareness.

The first step in learning how to use Dynamic Elemental Spreads is to define the five elements. We each get to define these elements any way we want. It doesn't matter how we define them. It doesn't matter if we're the only person in the world that defines the elements in this way. What matters is that we really understand what these definitions mean to us. These definitions are the vocabulary we'll use to communicate with our own subconscious mind. We're just using tarot cards to help our conscious and subconscious minds communicate.

## 2

Hopefully you have some key words, phrases, or concepts you've decided to use for each of the five elements. In this section of the chapter we're going to examine the possibilities for assigning each element to one of the five tarot suits. In section three we'll define the Dynamic Elemental Spreads and start reading.

AIR. Air is usually assigned to the suit of Swords but several authors assign Air to the suit of Wands. In some decks other things like daggers, birds, or flying things are used instead of Swords. Air is generally considered to be a masculine element. Your assignment is to look at your tarot deck and decide what suit best fits the Air element for you.

FIRE. Fire is usually assigned to the suit of Wands but several authors assign Fire to the suit of Swords. In some decks things like rods, staffs, or batons are used instead of Wands. Fire is generally considered to be a masculine element. Your assignment is to look at your tarot deck and decide what suit best fits the Fire element for you.

WATER. Water is generally assigned to the suit of Cups. Caldrons, rivers, lakes, chalices, and other containers are used in some decks instead of Cups. Water is considered to be a feminine suit. Your assignment is to look at your deck and decide what suit best fits the Water element for you.

EARTH. Earth is generally assigned to the suit of Pentacles. Coins, disks, trees or other plants, and land are used in some decks instead of Earth. Earth is considered to be a feminine suit. Your assignment is to look at your tarot deck and decide what suit best fits the Earth element for you.

SPIRIT. Spirit is generally assigned to the Major Arcana. Your assignment is to look at your tarot deck and decide what suit best fits the Spirit element for you.

In the next section we'll take up the third step, which is defining Dynamic Elemental Spreads. In the meantime, I suggest you spend some time assigning the elements to the tarot suits the way you want them assigned.

3

In section one we considered several options for defining the elements. In section two we examined possible ways of assigning each element to one of the five tarot suits. In this section we'll define the Dynamic Elemental Spreads and start reading.

To understand this section you'll need to know what suits are assigned to which elements and you'll need to know the definitions for the elements.

Step one: State your question in any form that can be answered by the tarot cards. Do not ask any ridiculous or unanswerable questions. It's easier if you state your question starting with what, when, which, why, where, who, or how. I suggest you write down your question exactly as you want it anytime you read for yourself. In the beginning, this is a good idea for all your readings until you become proficient.

Step two: Decide which element best reflects the essence of the question. Some questions span more than one element. That's fine, just make a note of it. It's not a problem. Then choose one element for the first reading. (You can choose other elements for subsequent readings.)

Step three: Mix the cards in any way you choose and select one card from the deck using any method of choice you desire. It's not important how you do these things. What's important is that you select a method and verbalize it so your emotional, intuitive, and subconscious minds all know what you're going to do.

Step four: Continue this process until you select a card of the same element as the question. Set aside all the other cards (face up) in a separate pile at this time. You may or may not use them as part of your reading.

Step five: Write down the card drawn and the meaning of this card if you're a beginner or if you're doing this reading for yourself. If you're already a tarot reader, make a mental note of the card drawn and its meaning.

Step six: Tune in to this card and use it to answer your question. If you're a beginner or doing this reading for yourself, I suggest you write out your reading for this card.

Step seven: If you need further clarification, use the top card in your discard pile. If you don't have a discard pile (the first card you drew was the element you were seeking) use this as a sign the answer is ambiguous at this time. If necessary, you can use the next cards, from top to bottom, in the discard pile to help explain the answer to your question.

I pay special attention to any Spirit cards in my discard pile. I've developed a relationship with my subconscious mind to always tell me what I need to know all the time. I've come to expect my own subconscious mind to communicate to me through this discard pile. It's funny, but it seems every time a Spirit card appears in my discard pile it brings an important message to me. When I'm doing a reading for another person, the Spirit card is an important message for him or her and not me.

Your assignment for this section is to play with this concept and see if you don't think this is a powerful way of doing one-card readings. In the next section I'll share a few examples with you to demonstrate how easy and accurate this system really is.

# 4

Let's go through some examples of Dynamic Elemental Spreads together.

Client number one asked: "When will I get a job offer?"

My process is to first decide which element is expressed by the question. In this system, jobs and careers are Fire and Fire is represented by Wands. The cards drawn for this reading, in order, were Page of Coins, The Moon, The Tower, The Magician, Ten of Wands. In this system, the Ten of Wands means carrying a heavy load. The answer to this person's question is: "As soon as you stop carrying a heavy load."

My client asked for clarification. The top card in my discard pile was The Magician which in this system means one needs to pay attention to his or her spiritual path. So I told my client: "The Magician card in this reading indicates you need to pay attention to your spiritual path and then all things will come to you." She said she understood exactly what the cards were telling her. That pleased me because the next card in the pile is a big "wake-up" call. Sometimes I wonder if that card is for me (he said as he chuckled to himself).

Client number two asked: "Is Tom the right one for me?"

Using the process being explained, I use Cups for Water and Water is relationships. The cards drawn for this reading were the Four of Swords and the Four of Cups. The Four of Cups in the system I'm using means "Love in spite of all other emotions." I told my client: "Tom loves you for who and what you are." She said: "Yes, but is he the right one for me?"

I looked at the only card in my discard pile and told her: "The Four of Swords means Love in spite of all thoughts and ideas to the contrary." She agreed that explained Tom very well: "But, is he the right one for me?" My response was: "These two cards tell me he is, yes, because he loves you in spite of negative thoughts and emotions." She wasn't convinced.

I said: "Let's draw another card. If that card's upright, the answer is yes; but if it's inverted, the answer is no. I turned the next card. It was the Knight of Cups which in the system being used means one who brings love into your life." I explained this to her. She smiled and said: "I thought so, but I just wanted confirmation."

Client number three asked: "Will my mother recover from her surgery?" Surgery is an Earth question for me. I drew the following cards: Justice, Five of Swords, High Priestess, Page of Coins. The Page in this system represents a person who brings good health to you. I explained to my client the Page represented a person who was helping her mother recover. So the answer to her question is "Yes, the cards believe your mother will recover from this surgery." Then I gave her all the disclaimers explaining how health questions should be answered by competent medical practitioners.

My client saw the High Priestess face up on the table and asked if that was a good omen. My response was yes, the High Priestess is a card of spiritual balance and that's a good omen. She agreed. Later that week she called to say her mother was recovering just fine. It's nice to get confirmation once in a while.

Client number four asked me to do a reading for her son who was recently arrested. I really don't like to do readings for a third party because you never know if there really is a third party or not. I explained that reading for somebody who isn't present at the reading is difficult but she kept saying: "Please!" I drew the following cards: Nine of Cups reversed, Death, Three of Swords, The Devil reversed. The Devil card in this system is a card of bondage, of being tied down to the affairs of this world. When reversed it often indicates addictions of one kind or another. I explained this to my client. She sat there without saying a word.

Usually in this situation I just wait until the client responds. But this time, I pointed to the Three of Swords and told her that card often means somebody's heart is being broken. She said it was her heart because her son was caught selling drugs to kids to pay for his own habit. Then she asked if there was anything else I could add. I looked at the next card and told her that her son was in for a big change in his life and that change would be beneficial for all concerned. She agreed he was in for a big change and hoped I was right about it being beneficial. But she wanted to know why I thought it would be beneficial. My answer was because the Death card was right side up. If it had been upside down the changes might not be all that good.

Client number five is me. I asked the cards what I needed to know about my diet. The card I drew was the inverted Strength card. In the system I was using, the Strength card means you have the strength to see it through. Inverted it means this is a problem to be addressed. What this means to me is the problem I need to face is not my diet but my weakness for food. Once I tackle this problem the diet will take care of itself.

Pure words of wisdom and I knew it. It sure dampened my enthusiasm for eating a piece of cake for lunch. But the message was loud and clear. It usually is whenever I ask the cards anything.

I hope these examples help you gain a little more confidence in your own tarot reading skills. In the next section we'll look a little more closely at Dynamic Elemental one-card Spreads.

## 5

I've been experimenting with the "I am One" Tarot deck these past two weeks. Here are a few readings I've done for myself and others:

Q – What effect will the proposed talisman have on prospective students?

A – Reversed Knight Two Headed Serpent (Fire) whose motto is: "I am Authority of Energy." This talisman is intended to increase the self-esteem of the students in a class I'm teaching on peak performance. The reading tells me the energy will help them improve their self-esteem and thus improve their performance. I went ahead and created this talisman.

Q – What effect will this ritual have on my friend?

A – Eight of Two Headed Serpent (Fire) whose key phrase is: "I am swift passage." This means things will move rather quickly once the ritual is completed. I completed the ritual. Within twenty-four hours she was called for an interview. The interview went very well. We'll have to wait a couple of weeks for the final outcome. She's been looking for a better position for at least the past six months.

Q – If I buy a new car right now, will I be able to afford it?
A – (Yes, this is the actual question.) Nine of Curved Blade (Air), Knight of Curved Blade, Reversed Queen of Two Headed Serpent (Fire), and the Reversed Six Stone of Age (Earth) which means "success." Reversed, this card means: "not success." My interpretation was that unless things changed, she wouldn't be able to afford it. She indicated that's what she thought but she just wanted confirmation.

The basic Dynamic Elemental Spread uses five positions, one for each of the five elements. The process is to prepare the deck in the manner you prefer, choose the cards in any manner you desire, and keep pulling cards until you have one card in each of the five suits. Place subsequent cards in the same suit on top of the card or cards already pulled in that suit. Here's a sample reading:

Q – If the president declares war against Iraq, what will happen to my son (he's in the National Guard)?
Spirit = Key 14 (The Reverser), Key 12 (The Hanging Man)
Fire = Seven of Two Headed Serpent
Water = Nine, Queen Pear of Tears
Air = One Curved Blade (last card drawn)
Earth = Knight, Seven, Two, Eight Stone of Age

Key 12 is the Master Redeemer. The Seven of Two Headed Serpent calls for evaluation of the situation before taking action. The Queen Pear of Tears is the Authority of Reason in all emotional situations. One Curved Blade is news. The Eight Stone of Age is Magnetism. My reading was at this time that the cards indicate her son will receive news regarding the war and be drawn into it. He will handle difficult situations well and return victorious.

If further information is needed about any one element, the cards beneath the top card can be used for that purpose. In the reading given, no further information was needed. She already knew her son was on alert and could be going to the Middle East at a minute's notice. She was glad to hear he would survive and return home.

Any question can be answered by the basic Dynamic Elemental Spread. The reader can either select the element that best answers the question or let the cards select the element based on the cards drawn.

One way is to select the last card drawn. Another is to select the top card in the pile with the most cards.

A third way of using the Dynamic Elemental Spread is to first decide what element will best answer the question being asked. Then draw one card using the selection process of your choice. Interpret this card as though it were in the element desired. If it actually is, then give the reading added emphasis. Here's an example:

Q – What will happen if I ask the boss for a raise next week?

A – I decided this was an Earth question. The card drawn was the Seven of Cups which means Delusion or Illusion. Interpreted in terms of Earth, this means to me the raise in question is an illusion. The fact the card drawn was Cups also indicated this is an emotional issue with my client. After sharing this insight we discussed other options for additional income besides asking for a raise that probably won't materialize. During this discussion I learned he'd asked for a raise a couple of times and been turned down. He didn't think there was much chance this time either.

You might want to play with several variations of the Dynamic Elemental Spreads to see which one works best for you, or create your own variation. In the next section we'll take a look at some ways of answering "When" questions.

## 6

"When" questions as a group are difficult for most beginners and even some experts. The Dynamic Elemental Spreads offer one way of answering "When" questions efficiently and effectively. The rules are easy to remember:

Rule Number One: Decide which element is expressed by the question. This requires you to have good definitions for the types of things related to each element. If the question is about the client's work, you need to decide if this is an emotional issue (Water) or an intellectual one (Air). It may simply be a work question which you need to assign to either Fire or Earth.

Rule Number Two:  Prepare the deck in any way you decide. Draw cards from the deck using the method of your choice. Keep drawing cards and placing them in piles according to their element until you draw a card of the element expressed by the question. This is the last card you'll draw from the deck.

Rule Number Three:  The last card drawn is the answer to the question as to when something will happen. It will happen just as soon as the event depicted by the card drawn occurs. Time is irrelevant. When the client does what the card advises him or her to do, the desired event will occur.

Rule Number Four:  The cards drawn prior to the final card depict events which will also need to occur, but not necessarily in the order drawn. Here's an example using the Rider-Waite-Smith deck.

My client asked "When will I find a job?" which I took to be a Fire question (career). The cards drawn (by element in the order drawn) were:

Spirit:  Hierophant, Tower reversed
Water:  Six of Cups
  Fire:  Four of Wands reversed (last card)

In the system being used the fours have to do with love and the sixes with balance of the emotions. The Hierophant is Intuition and the reversed Tower is a call to wake up. Reversed Wands refers to intuitive insights. My interpretation was: As soon as you start listening to your intuitive insights, you'll find a job you love. In order to do this you'll need to become less emotional about finding a job—balance your mind, heart, and spirit. You'll also need to wake up and listen to your intuition.

The client discussed these issues with me. She agreed she dismisses her intuitive insights as false beliefs and illusions of grandeur. She agreed she's started to panic about a job and she believes this panic has scared off a couple of prospective employers. She asked for help in overcoming her fears and we created an amulet to help keep away these negative feelings of fear and panic. (Yes, the moon was waxing and I broke one of Donald Michael Kraig's suggested rules for amulets.

But in his book Don gave us all permission to break the rules.) She also identified the kind of job she'd really like to have. In my experience, knowing what you really want is the first step in attaining it.

This wasn't a one-card tarot reading, but it could have been done that way. The first three cards drawn could have been ignored and I could have used only the inverted Four of Wands to answer her question. If she asked for further clarification, I could use the other cards or just the second to last card drawn. This raises an interesting question about how to keep track of both the element and the sequence of the cards.

I do it by laying the cards out in five columns and placing the second card on top of the first so both cards can be identified. You might think of this as setting up five columns of solitaire. I have Spirit on the left followed by Fire, Water, Air, and Earth in that order. That works for me. I have no idea what will work best for you. But the good news is you can figure that all out for yourself.

Your assignment for this section is to try answering a few "When" questions using the approach suggested here. Then for extra credit you can create your own method for answering "When" questions. In the next section we'll take a look at some ways of answering "How" and "Why" questions.

# 7

"How" and "Why" questions are answered in much the same way as "When" questions using the Dynamic Elemental Spreads. The rules for responding to "How" and "Why" questions are modified only slightly from those given in the last section for "When" questions:

Rule Number One: Decide which element is expressed by the question.

Rule Number Two: Prepare the deck and draw cards from the deck using the method of your choice. Keep drawing cards and placing them in piles according to their element until you draw a card of the element expressed by the question.

Rule Number Three: The last card drawn is the answer to the question and any cards drawn prior to the final card may be used to further clarify this answer.

To do a one-card reading, use only the last card drawn, the one of the element chosen for this reading. Any other cards drawn for this reading may be used for clarification purposes or ignored. Interpret the card drawn according to the system you choose to use and give the reading accordingly. You may expect the card to explain exactly how or why the event mentioned in the question is occurring. It's up to you to use this explanation to answer the question.

Alternatively, the top card for each element may be used to do a more complete reading. Again, any cards beneath the top card can be used for clarification purposes. This technique will result in a reading of one to five elements depending upon how many cards were drawn for each element before the element being sought to answer the question. You may not have drawn a card for one or more of the elements.

The basic Dynamic Elemental Spread, where cards are drawn until each of the five elements has at least one card representing it, can be used to give a five-card reading over all of the elements. You may also choose to use any number of elements for your reading. My only suggestion is to choose the elements before you draw any cards to answer the question. That way you keep the lines of communication open with your own subconscious mind.

Q – Why is (blank) treating me this way? (I'll consider this a Water question.)

The cards drawn are:

Key VIII Strength = you have the fortitude to do it.
Four of Wands reversed = love intuitive insights.
Key V Hierophant = intuition.
Five of Cups = anger in relationships.

This last card is the one I'm looking for. It tells me she's angry with me in our relationship. OK, she's angry. Now what? Well, the previous cards tell me to use my intuition, love those intuitive insights, and rely on my own strength to resolve this issue.

Gee, that worked out so well it almost looks contrived. But I really did draw the cards at random and I was looking for an answer and I got one. I'm going to ask the same question about another person who's treating me with great respect and attending to my every wish. Let's see how that comes out.

Q – Why is (blank) treating me this way? (I'll consider this a Water question too.)

The cards drawn are:

Inverted Six of Pentacles = desire in material things.
Inverted Three of Pentacles = understand material things.
Inverted King of Wands = verify intuitive insights.
Wheel of Fortune = what goes around, comes around.
Inverted Page of Cups = justice in friendships.

The inverted Page of Cups tells me she's treating me fairly as a friend in the manner in which she sees me treating her. Our friendship is emotionally balanced. The other cards can help me clarify this answer. The definitions of these cards speak for themselves.

Q – How can I resolve the financial issues for (blank company)? (I'll consider this an Earth question.)

The cards drawn are:

Key XIX The Sun = illumination.
Inverted Ace of Cups = beginning of a friendship.
Two of Cups = intention to create a relationship.
Key X Wheel of Fortune = what goes around, comes around.
Inverted Page of Wands = intuition is right.
Inverted Knight of Cups = change in thinking about the friendship.
Queen of Pentacles = change in behavior regarding money.

There's the rub. The company needs to change their behavior regarding money. This means they need to change the way they handle their financial affairs. To clarify this issue, look at the previous cards going back in order. They need to change their thinking about their friendship with money. They need to trust their intuitive insights and know that what they do with money is how money will treat them. They've been using money to create relationships.

As I study this spread, I've got to tell you it's so true but I've never looked at this company in that light before. They have been trying to "buy friends" in the world of commerce. That never works. All you ever do is spend money and receive little or nothing in return. That leads me to the next question.

Q – How do I tell them (the above company) these things? (It's still an Earth question.)

The cards drawn are:

Key XX Judgement = rebirth.
Two of Pentacles = money intentions.

This one is a little more difficult and requires some thought. The phrase "money intentions" means to look at what you really want to accomplish, what your real intentions are. This tells me to approach the officers with this question for analysis. Out of this will come a "rebirth" in the way which they choose to use their money. I peeked at the first card for a little bit of clarification.

Aftermath: I won't go into a lot of detail, but I did exactly as the cards suggested. The officers agreed they needed to change the way they've been spending a lot of money and they're setting up new spending policies. It's a change from feeding the "Good Old Boys Network" to more intelligently prospecting for customers. The net result will be a saving of a considerable amount of money they couldn't afford in the first place. Intuitively, I feel they'll have a lot more success with their new marketing approach.

Your assignment for this section, should you choose to try it, is to do several "How" and "Why" tarot spreads to answer questions for yourself and your friends. In the next section we'll take a look at some ways of answering "Who, What, Where, and Which" questions.

## 8

"Who, What, Where, and Which" questions are answered the same way as "How" and "Why" questions using the Dynamic Elemental Spreads. The rules for responding to "Who, What, Where, and Which" questions are repeated here for your convenience:

Rule Number One:  Decide which element is expressed by the question.

Rule Number Two:  Prepare the deck and draw cards from the deck using the method of your choice. Keep drawing cards and placing them in piles according to their element until you draw a card of the element expressed by the question.

Rule Number Three:  The last card drawn is the answer to the question and any cards drawn prior to the final card may be used to further clarify this answer.

To do a one-card reading, use only the last card drawn, the one of the element chosen for this reading. Any other cards drawn for this reading may be used for clarification purposes or ignored. Interpret the card drawn according to the system you choose to use and give the reading accordingly. You may expect the card to explain exactly how or why the event mentioned in the question is occurring. It's up to you to use this explanation to answer the question.

Alternatively, the top card for each element may be used to do a more complete reading. Again, any cards beneath the top card can be used for clarification purposes. This technique will result in a reading of one to five elements depending upon how many cards were drawn for each element before the element being sought to answer the question. You may not have drawn a card for one or more of the elements.

The basic Dynamic Elemental Spread, where cards are drawn until each of the five elements has at least one card representing it, can be used to give a five-card reading over all of the elements. You may also choose to use any number of elements for your reading. My only suggestion is to choose the elements before you draw any cards to answer the question. That way you keep the lines of communication open with your own subconscious mind.

Q – Who's going to get the job I applied for?
A – Inverted Two of Swords = attitude of determination.

This person knows what they want and projects that attitude for all to see. That's the person who'll get the job you applied for. (It turned out to be the client who was the "attitude of determination" person.) The essence of all "Who" answers is that the card describes an important, easy-to-recognize characteristic about the person in question.

Q – What's the best way for me to learn tarot?
A – Inverted Devil = become free of all preconceptions.

This card tells it all. Forget everything you know and think you know. Let the cards teach you how to read them. All "What" questions receive a direct and succinct answer.

Q – Where will I find my soul mate? (same client)
A – Inverted Strength = weakness.

The place where you find yourself most vulnerable is the place of your weakness and that's where you'll find your soul mate.

Q – Which place? A, B, or C? (same client, yet again)
A – Inverted High Priestess = lack of direction.

At this point I checked my deck to see if the whole thing was upside down Major Arcana. The deck was fine. The answer was "the place where you feel a complete lack of direction." The client said that was option C because she couldn't find her way around that area at all but she knew the other two areas quite well. Then she said something that professional tarot readers hear a lot: "I thought so, but I just needed confirmation."

Your assignment this week, should you choose to try it, is to do several "What, Who, Where, and Which" tarot spreads to answer questions for yourself and your friends. In the next section we'll take a look at some ways of answering "Is, Are?" and "Yes/No" questions.

## 9

Questions beginning with "is" or "are" requiring a yes or no answer can be handled a number of ways. The easiest system to use is inverted cards for no and upright cards for yes.

Q – Am I doing the right thing for me to (blank)?
A – Inverted Six of Cups = No, you're not. To which my client responded: "I thought so." Professional tarot readers can make a lot of money confirming that their client's intuitive insights are correct.

The second easiest method of answering yes/no questions is to use the even-numbered cards for yes and the odd-numbered cards for no.

Q – Am I going to get this job with (blank)?
A – Inverted Six of Cups (six = yes).

Actually, the card was upright, but my point is that only the number is critical in arriving at the answer using this numerical method of answering yes/no questions.

Q – Am I doing all right with my readings?
A – Inverted Key XVI The Tower = awakening.

The Tower card is not often seen as positive in many systems, but here the answer is "yes" because sixteen is an even number. Additionally, the card tells me you're having difficulty awakening to the fact you're doing just fine with your tarot readings. My suggestion is to keep on reading and believe in yourself. At least, believe in your higher self.

Another way is to use the feminine suits of Water and Earth for yes and the masculine suits of Fire and Air for no. This can be called the Elemental Approach while the previous one could be called the Numerical Approach. Using this system the Major Arcana cards say "I don't know yet" or "maybe yes, maybe no." And the card drawn also explains why no answer is yet available, or why the answer isn't available to your client. That's tricky, but it works.

Q – Did (blank) steal the money from the company?
A – This is the kind of question I really don't like to answer for a number of reasons. What if I'm wrong? Or maybe interpret a card wrongly? What's going to happen to (blank) based on my answer? What kind of karma am I creating for myself? What's my client going to do with this information? Is it ethical to even try to answer such a question?

So my standard response is something to the effect that the cards don't invade the privacy of other people. In this case, my client wouldn't let it go. Against my better judgement, and I certainly don't recommend you or anybody ever does anything against his or her better judgement, I pulled the inverted Judgement card. Was this card for me? Or my client?

That's the first thought that crossed my mind. This card means Rebirth to me. Inverted it indicates a major issue in the individual's life.

I explained to my client the tarot won't say yes or no. What it does say is blank's going through a major crisis in blank's life and the change will be dramatic, like being born again. Several days later I called my client to ask how things came out. She explained the employee came to her, confessed everything, and made full restitution. That sounded like a crisis and rebirth situation to me. Was I just lucky? Maybe!

Q – Is March a good time for me to start a part-time business reading tarot cards?

A – Queen of Cups = yes (Water). In this case, the Queen also says a lot about this person's abilities. That's often the case using either of these two methods of handling yes/no questions.

Q – Do your cards think this is a good time for me to move in with (blank)?

A – Inverted Seven of Cups (Water = yes).

Yes, but my cards also caution you to see things as they are and not how you think they should be.

Your assignment this week, should you choose to try it, is to do several "Is, Are?" and "Yes/No" tarot spreads to answer questions for yourself and your friends. In the next section we'll wrap up these discussions of Dynamic Elemental Spreads.

## 10

Either/or questions can be handled as yes/no questions by rephrasing the question. Another way is to assign the upright cards to option one and the inverted cards to option two. I used this variation several weeks ago:

Q – Should I do the (blank) ritual today or wait and do it later?

I assumed upright cards to indicate "now," inverted to "later," and decided that I would delay the ritual one day for each inverted card I drew. The cards drawn were:

Inverted Six of Wands = later
Inverted Two of Cups = later
Inverted Moon = later

Inverted Ace of Swords = later
Ten of Pentacles = this day, five days later.

An interesting aside is that day five just happened to be February 16, a full moon day. Special rituals tend to work better for me if started on the new or full moon or first and third quarter moons. My regular rituals seem to work better for me if done just before sunrise. I don't have any idea what will work best for you. But the good news is you can experiment and discover the answer for yourself.

Q – What do the cards say in respect to these two men in my life at this time or is there another prospect on the way?

A – In answer to "Is there another prospect on the way?" the card drawn was the Seven of Pentacles. Yes, there's another prospect on the way if you want to wait for him or her to appear in your life.

In answer to the first question, the card for Man #1 was the inverted Devil. He has a problem being tied down in life and enjoys his freedom to be and do what he wants when he wants to be and do it.

The card for Man #2 is The Hierophant. He's a man of habits who likes to do things in a set routine. You can expect him to do what he's always done.

In answer as to which one is the better choice for you right now the card was inverted Nine of Swords. This indicates Man #2 is the better choice but it's not an easy choice for you to make. In answer as to whether the unknown prospect would be a better choice than Man #2, the card drawn was the inverted Ace of Pentacles. No, he would not be a better choice at this time. Good luck.

You'll notice I ended up doing four separate one-card readings for this compound question. One of my own rules for doing tarot readings is "One question at a time." That means I normally break compound questions up into two or more questions and answers.

A second rule is to answer the unasked question hidden within the question actually being asked. In this case, she didn't specifically ask which man was a better choice, but that question underlay the one she did ask.

This concludes our discussion of Dynamic Elemental Spreads. My hope is you've found something to help you along the way. Your assignment, should you choose to do it, is to continue experimenting with various questions using the Dynamic Elemental Spreads.

# CHAPTER 5

# Tarot and numerology

## 1

Numerology is an ancient divination method that has been used with tarot for a long time. The following list gives you one traditional way to understand the first ten numbers:

0 – before the beginning
1 – Beginnings, awareness
2 – Expansion, intention
3 – Drawing inward, beliefs
4 – Getting organized, evaluation
5 – Changes, crisis
6 – Peace, harmony
7 – Learning from mistakes, success
8 – Preparation for an ending, reevaluation
9 – Endings, end of a cycle

What do these words mean? Let's take them one at a time.

0 – Before the beginning. Before the beginning we were all a part of the Creator. We were not separate from the Creator and we were not

separate from each other. We were all together in the celestial "Garden of Eden." As a result of the creation we were given the opportunity to exercise our free will and become a part of the creation or to remain a part of the Creator.

The fact that we're here in this physical reality is a testament to the fact we chose to become a part of the creation. We chose to become incarnated in this physical body. Not only did we choose to become incarnated, we chose our body. We chose our body exactly the way it is. Not only did we choose it, we created it. We participated in the creation of this physical reality by creating our own body.

Not only did we create our physical body, we created our mental, emotional, and psychological bodies as well. We created the person we are in this reality. We did that for a purpose and that purpose is our primary reason for existing in the physical reality.

The number zero represents everything before this beginning. It is the time before a creation during which the creator decides what to create. It was the time before our physical creation when we decided what to create. It was the time before we were born into this physical reality.

1 – Awareness. Once we are born into this physical reality, the first thing we are able to do is pay attention to this new and strange world around us. We become aware of our surroundings. That's all we can do, become aware. We can't change anything in our environment. We can't do anything but become aware. Our body runs itself and we pay attention. We become aware. Until we become aware we are helpless, without direction, confused, and unable to do anything. The first step in creating anything is awareness.

2 – Intention. Having become aware we start to decide we want certain things or we want certain things to happen. These certain things are our intentions. We intend to be fed. We intend to be clean and clothed in dry clothing. We intend to be held. We intend to be loved. Intention is the mother of invention. Without intentions we are aimless and subject to the whims of others. Our intentions are a necessary step in the creative process.

3 – Belief. Our intentions can multiply forever. There is no limit to the number of intentions we can conceive. There is no limit except for our beliefs. Our beliefs that we can or cannot do something limit our ability to create. Our beliefs also focus our intentions so we can create that which we believe we can. Our beliefs are both a necessity and a blessing.

4 – Order. We organize ourselves as our intentions become manifested within our belief system. We organize our intentions. We organize our beliefs. We organize that which we're creating. We bring order out of the chaos of creation.

5 – Crisis. But no matter how well we organize and plan, the unexpected happens and we have a crisis. We're not prepared for this crisis but it happens anyway. This is typical of the growth of all new things. The first five steps are predictable once we have an intention to do anything.

6 – Harmony. We either weather the crisis and survive or we fail. If we fail, we must come to grips with our failure and move on. If we weather the crisis and survive, we must move on. This is the balance point, the point of no return. From here we either move on to the next step in the process or we go back to the beginning and do it all over again.

7 – Success. Success is learning from our mistakes. If we do not learn from our mistakes, we do not succeed. We may succeed but our creation may fail. That's when we learn the most important lesson of all – that what we do is not important, who we are is the only important thing.

8 – Evaluation. We now begin to evaluate both our intentions and our beliefs about our intentions. We evaluate strengths and weaknesses and we evaluate our progress toward realizing our intentions. This evaluation either moves us forward or backward to the beginning.

9 – Ending. The end of a cycle comes as soon as we evaluate our failures and successes. This ending is not final. We continue on with a new beginning and repeat this cycle time after time until we learn all the lessons we came here to learn.


## 2

With all this in mind, our first task in using numerology with tarot will be to define the four elements and assign each of them to a suit in our deck.

Earth normally means money and material things and is represented by coins, disks, or pentacles. But you may define Earth to mean anything you want it to be and may assign any suit of your choice to it.

Air normally means thinking (airheads think a lot!), ideas, and thoughts. It can also mean philosophy, dreaming and daydreaming, or concerns and nightmares. Air is usually represented by swords or spears but you may choose any suit to be Air.

Water usually means love and friendship, emotions and caring, and is represented by cups or caldrons. Again, you may assign any meaning and any suit to Water.

Fire usually represents psychic energy or intuitive insights, internal drive and will, or even careers. The suit of Fire is often wands, rods, staves, or other blunt weapons.

Notice that wands and swords can both be weapons and thus represent the masculine or more aggressive part of life. Water and Earth represent softer more feminine attributes to life.

Your task, should you choose to undertake it, is to assign one of the elements to each suit of your tarot deck and define what that suit, and element, will mean for you. Once you've done this you're ready to proceed to the numbers.

The number one is the first number and it represents the first step in any undertaking. One is a beginning. It's a new source of income, a new boy toy or a new girlie thing, a new idea, a new way of thinking, a new relationship, a new love, an intuitive insight, a new career, or a new job. One is a birth, a child, a pet, a loved one.

One is the first thing that happens to an element. It's the creative influence of the universe expressed in Earth, Air, Water, and Fire. Since you already know what you want the elements to mean for you, all you need to do now is decide what a beginning means for that element and the aces in your tarot deck. That's the first step to assigning a meaning, a phrase, a word, a concept to each card in your tarot deck. Forget what everybody else does or is doing. Do it your way and it'll work for you.

## 3

The number one is the seed of all things, the seed of income, ideas, relationships, feelings, intuition, employment, and everything else. As a seed first puts down a root before it expands into the world so does the number two. In fact if you look at the number "2" it has the most solid foundation of any number. It is well grounded. It is well rooted and ready to expand. It is balanced and stands tall.

Just as the root balances the seed so it can send up a strong upright shoot, so the number two balances all it touches. Without this strong grounding, this balance, the tree would lean to one side or the other and it would not be balanced. It would not be upright and it would not be strong.

The number two takes what has been started with the number one and makes it grow in a balanced manner, a controlled and balanced growth. Whatever it is, it grows to be twice as big as it was in the beginning for two is twice as big as one. And as it grows it maintains a balance between opposites, opposites like left and right, north and south, up and down, east and west, light and dark, positive and negative, male and female.

The number two is thus interpreted as steady growth, balance, addition, well-grounded, firm foundation, and many other things. All you need to do is decide what the number two will mean for you. Write it down so you won't forget. Memorize this meaning and then apply it to the five twos in your tarot deck.

## 4

If the number one is the seed and two the root then number three is the tree, the upward shoot. It represents the addition of one, the seed, and two, the root or the foundation of the thing.

If number one is the beginning and two the addition of the thing, then three is its multiplication. One root goes down from the seed and expands. One branch goes up from the seed and expands. Thus both two and three expand, but three expands faster. Three expands faster because it has a firm foundation. This is multiplication.

The number three takes what has been begun by the number one, expanded by the number two and multiplies it, expands it faster and further than before. It moves the energy outward in all directions. This is fruitfulness. This is being fruitful.

The number three is thus interpreted as being rapid expansion, rapid growth, multiplication, fruitfulness, and many other things. All you need to do is decide what the number three will mean for you. Write it down so you won't forget. Memorize this meaning and then apply it to the five threes in your tarot deck.

We've just passed the halfway point in applying numerology to your tarot deck. You now have eight key words, phrases, or concepts for your tarot deck: one for each of the five elements and one for each of the first three numbers. With only six more numbers to go, we're already more than half done.

## 5

Continuing our story about the seed (One) which sprouts a root or foundation (Two) and then expands upward (Three) we next form a tree (Four).

Four represents the forming of a tree, the organization of the parts of the tree to make the whole. Four represents the making of bark, leaves, and limbs. It's the number of getting organized, of making order out of the chaos of growth. It's the number of structure because the trunk and limbs form the structure upon which the leaves can grow. It's the number of manifestation.

The number four is the number of form, organization, structure, and manifestation. It also represents the "squaring of things," of making them right. Masons square their actions by the compass and the square. That means they walk a straight line and follow the rules.

Decide what the number four will mean for you. Write it down so you won't forget. Memorize this meaning and then apply it to the five fours in your tarot deck. Only five more numbers to go!

## 6

We started our analogy of a tree with the seed which has since sprouted, and developed a root system, trunk, and branches. Taking this one step further, the tree blossoms into myriad leaves and flowers. The energy once contained within the small seed is now seemingly multiplying without end.

This expansive multiplication of energy is represented by the number five. But expansion without restriction may not be in our best interests. He or she who expands spending money without limit becomes the Five of Pentacles. He or she who indulges in anything too much becomes the Five of Cups. Those who want everything take too much of what doesn't belong to them and become the Five of Swords. And those who become too self-centered encourage conflict and become the Five of Wands. Thus too much expansion leads to misfortune.

More than anything else the number five indicates we have gone overboard, expanded too much, and caused ourselves discomfort in the process. Too much energy without any controls causes us problems. That's the message of the fives. Decide what key word, phrase, or concept you will use for the number five.

It's time to practice with all the cards you've defined so far. They are 0, I, II, III, IV, V, aces, twos, threes, fours, and fives. Later you'll see where we also include X, XI, XII, XIII, XIV, XIX, XX, XXI, tens, Pages (11), Knights (12), Queens (13), and Kings (14) in the numbers from one through five. We do this by thinking of these higher numbers (above nine) as higher expressions of the base number obtained by adding the digits of the number. For example, the base number for 14 is $1 + 4 = 5$ and for the number 12 it's $1 + 2 = 3$ for our purposes.

You might want to play with these concepts and see what you think. We've four more numbers to go and then we'll try to make this into a quick and easy system for learning to read the tarot.

## 7

Five is a number of expansion beyond all containment. It's spending too much money (Pentacles), thinking about things too much (Swords), having too many relationships (Cups), and spending too much energy (Wands). The tree has flowered and grown leaves abundantly.

Now the tree stops growing, the leaves turn from green to other colors and it becomes a thing of living beauty. This beauty, this harmony is represented by the number six. The energy has stopped expanding and harmony prevails. Now we spend only what we need and have money to share (Pentacles), we think about things less and find happiness in memories (Swords), we refrain from so many relationships and find joy in the ones we have (Cups), and we conserve some of our energy (Wands). We are in harmony with ourselves and our world.

Consider the number five and how it is expressed in Keys V and XIV. Consider the number six and see how it might be expressed in Key VI and Key XV. If it appears to you XIV relates better to six and XV better to five on first appearance, you're not alone.

But consider the spiritual equivalent of having too much spiritual energy. Couldn't that be XIV? Couldn't harmony with myself be expressed by XV as spiritual deprivation and too much ME? Hmm, that is food for thought, isn't it?

## 8

Our tree has grown from a seed to a fully mature plant. Its leaves have changed into beautiful fall colors and the time to withdraw has come. The tree turns and draws its outward growth into itself. The life's blood of the tree flows down from the limbs to the roots. This is how the tree will survive the coming cold months.

For us to survive the trials and tribulations of life we must do the same thing from time to time. We must withdraw from the outer world and go within. This introspection is an act of inner growth rather than outer, but it is growth nonetheless.

As we look inside ourselves we learn the lessons and integrate the knowledge into ourselves. It becomes a part of us and we become the better for it. Do not confuse this inner growth with sloth or laziness. While outward appearances may suggest this, inner work is hard work. The battles you fight are just as real as the physical realities of life. It's just that all these battles are with your concept of reality (Pentacles), your feelings and emotions (Cups), your ideas (Swords), and your psychic impressions (Wands). So the number seven directs us to look inside ourselves and learn the lesson of the suit.

Key VII directs us to look inside ourselves to learn where we are spiritually in relationship to who and what we are. Key XVI does the same thing. How can this be so?

In Key VII we're on a spiritual quest to become all we can become and we stop to look inside to see how we're doing. We're going to do a little self-evaluation. After we analyze these results, we next decide what changes we want to make in our lives, if any.

In Key XVI it appears we've come to the same point in our lives. We're at a point where we need to reevaluate. So Key XVI suggests we go inside and do just that. Then we decide what changes we want to make in our lives. That's introspection and that's what the number seven is all about.

## 9

Our growing tree has reached a point in its life where it is about to set off on its last spurt of growth this season. That growth occurred on all the odd numbers associated with this cycle (one year) of being. The first growth stage was exemplified by the seed sprouting. The second stage was with the number three when the tree expanded in size considerably by sending up a trunk and branches. The third stage of growth was with the number five when the three expanded into branches and leaves beyond number. Each of these three growth spurts was greater than the preceding. Then with the number seven the tree went within to grow and this growth was less expansive than that associated with the number five. The growth to follow with the number nine will be even less expansive.

It's as though we grow a little, then a lot, then a whole lot, then a lot a second time but in a different manner, and finally just a little. After each growth stage we have a period of reorganization, a peaceful time of synthesizing our growth. That's what happened when we started out with complete peace as the zero, as we brought our life back into balance with the two, organized our life with the four, regained our peace with the six, and now prepare for a final stage of growth with the eight.

This final preparation for our final growth during this cycle is a time of pruning off those things we need to prune. A time of bringing together all we've learned so far and deciding what we still need to learn in this cycle. It's a time of peaceful recollection and remembering. It's also a time of continuing evaluation.

In the next chapter we'll complete this cycle of growth as our tree goes into a state of slow growth during the winter. Thus we complete one cycle and prepare to start another.

## 10

The number nine is usually considered to be an ending to a particular cycle. It's a time when this cycle comes to a close.

Using our analogy of the tree starting from a seed, sprouting, growing, and thriving during the summer months and getting ready for a rest during autumn, we now arrive at winter and the end of this year's cycle. The tree now rests and survives the winter months. A new cycle will begin in the spring, but right now the old cycle is ending.

There are cycles in our lives. We move through ups and downs and these are expressions of our financial, health, material cycles with Pentacles, emotional, romantic cycles with Cups, thought and attitude cycles with Swords, and intuitive, career or cycles of determination with Wands. These are the cycles in our lives.

The nine indicates the ending of a cycle. One will start the new cycle and we'll move step by step through the numbers to a new ending, and then the cycles will repeat. Some say forever. Others say until we learn the lessons we must learn. Still others say we move through one cycle and then another as long as we live. Thus we grow and mature. This is the message of the nines.

Shortly, we'll start putting this all together into a system for learning the tarot. The key is to learn one key word, phrase, or concept for each of the numbers one through nine and one key word, phrase, or concept for each of the five elements—Earth, Air, Water, Fire, and Spirit.

## 11

In the earlier sections of this chapter we've been examining one way of looking at numbers. There are many different systems and many different ways of defining the meanings of numbers. The best way is the way you design for yourself. If you don't know where to start, use your browser to search for "numerology." You'll find more than you need to get started.

Here's a quick and easy system based on our discussions so far:

1. Beginning, new
2. Balance, slow growth, addition
3. Expansion, fast growth, multiplication
4. Order, squaring things
5. Growing too fast, too much
6. Beauty, restoring balance
7. Inner growth, learning
8. Preparation for an ending
9. End of a cycle

Remember, this is only one way of doing it. There are many, many more approaches to numerology. Find one that works for you or build your own system. Building your own system is probably the best approach in the long run. Why? Because you can really become an expert of your own system.

Who do you suppose really understands the Robin Wood Tarot the best? Might it be Robin Wood herself? Hmm. Might you understand your own system better than anybody else? Might it work really well for you? All the time? Sure! Why not? You made it, you gave birth to it, you refined it and watched it grow, and it's a part of you. So, of course it really works well for you!

Now you need to define the meanings of the five suits. One way is like this:

Earth (Pentacles) – Finances and material things
Water (Cups) – Relationships
Air (Swords) – Thoughts and ideas
Fire (Wands) – Intuitive insights
Spirit (Keys) – Spiritual growth

If you want to use reversals, one way to approach them is to give each element a different definition if the card is reversed. For example:

Reversed Earth – Health
Reversed Water – Friendships
Reversed Air – Attitude
Reversed Fire – Career
Reversed Spirit – Problem with your spiritual path

Now all you have left to do is:

1. Define the meaning of zero
2. Define how to handle numbers greater than nine
3. Define how to handle the court cards
4. Write it all down, memorize it and use it

Zero can mean whatever you want it to mean. One way of looking at The Fool is "getting ready to start something" or "getting ready to start a spiritual journey."

The numbers greater than ten are usually reduced to one number by adding the digits together. For example, ten (10) is $1 + 0 = 1$ and is therefore a new ace. This time you have some experience behind you but it's still another beginning.

Fifteen (15) is $1 + 5 = 6$ so The Devil is a new way of looking at The Lovers (Key 6). Yes, I picked a tough one on purpose. Whatever The Lovers means to you, The Devil means the same thing but there's a lot more experience behind it. Therefore it can be a more important lesson, or another way of looking at things. How you define the "second harmonic" is up to you.

The term second harmonic means this is a higher, more spiritual way of looking at the same thing. There is a higher purpose, a higher vibration, a higher "whatever you want it to be."

The numerological assignment for the court cards is usually the next four numbers in the sequence. They are not interpreted as court cards but as a higher vibration of the number involved. Here's how:

Page = 11 which is a higher expression of 2
Knight = 12 which is a higher expression of 3
Queen = 13 which is a higher expression of 4
King = 14 which is a higher expression of 5

So if the Five of Pentacles is "Spending too much money" the King of Pentacles might be "Accumulating too much money." If the Four of Cups is "Bringing order to your relationship," the Queen of Cups might be "Being in control of your relationship." If the Three of Swords is "Too many ideas" the Knight of Swords might be "Really too many ideas, really unfocused." If the Two of Wands is "Balancing intuitive insights in your life," the Page of Wands might be "Making intuitive insights really work for you."

So if you lay the cards out in nine rows corresponding to your nine numbers (plus zero), you have the following arrangement:

0
1s, 10s, I, X, XIX
2s, Pages, II, XI, XX
3s, Knights, III, XII, XXI
4s, Queens, IV, XIII
5s, Kings, V, XIV
6s, VI, XV
7s, VII, XVI
8s, VIII, XVII
9s, IX, XVIII

The cards in the same row are all different expressions of the same basic number one through nine (plus zero). So, there you have it, a system for using numerology to understand your tarot cards. Your assignment now, if you choose to accept it, is to devise your own system for using numerology to understand your tarot cards. Good luck.

# CHAPTER 6

# Tarot and astrology

## 1

In this chapter we start a study of how astrology can help us understand the tarot cards and how to build a system around this knowledge. The first step in doing this is to define the ten planets and twelve signs of the zodiac. How you define these things is up to you. Each sign and planet has a lot of possible meanings. You only need one meaning for each to build a complete system.

You don't need to make this complex. Keep it simple. Use key words or phrases that make sense to you. Check around the internet for meanings other people assign to the signs and planets. Read a book or two about astrology. Write down the important things you learn about these things.

The only other thing you need to learn is what the aspects mean. We'll discuss these later, but the major aspects are the sextile, trine, square, opposition, and conjunction. If you want, you can also use the semisextile, quintile, and other aspects. Again, what you use and how you define them is up to you.

The twelve signs of the zodiac are often considered to be the twelve rays which the Divine uses to create all there is. In ancient times these twelve signs were the twelve tribes of Israel and the description of each sign was a description of the typical person who belonged to that tribe.

Times change. Things change. Today there are more meanings attributed to each sign of the zodiac than the average person can memorize in a lifetime. My suggestion to you is to find one meaning that "fits" for you and use it. Here's one way to do that:

Aries (The Ram) = Headstrong: "We'll do it my way!" (Fire)
Taurus (The Bull) = Stubborn: "No I won't change!" (Earth)
Gemini (Twins) = Sociable: "I love to be with people" (Air)
Cancer (Crab) = Maternal: "I love my memories!" (Water)

These are the first four signs of the zodiac. The first three represent spring and the fourth is the start of summer. They represent the first of three cycles of the elements through the zodiac.

Your assignment this week, if you choose to do it, is to find a key word or phrase for each of these signs that makes sense to you. Here's another way of looking at the first four signs by their motto and their way of looking at life:

Aries = I am (I do it my way)
Taurus = I possess (It's mine, all mine)
Gemini = I communicate (I think, therefore I talk)
Cancer = I belong (This is my family)

Start by deciding what key word, phrase, or concept you're going to use for the first four signs of the zodiac.

## 2

In the first section of this chapter we examined the first four signs of the Zodiac and gave you some ideas about what they mean. It was suggested you find a key word or phrase to describe each of these signs. This week, your assignment, if you choose to accept it, is to find a key word or phrase for each of the other eight signs. Here's one way to approach this subject:

Leo (The Lion) = Conceited "Nobody does it better" (Fire)
Virgo (The Virgin) = Servant "How may I serve you?" (Earth)
Libra (The Scales) = Indecisive "What should I do?" (Air)

Scorpio (Scorpion) = Emotional "I'll fight to the death" (Water)
Sagittarius (Centaur) = Independent "I'm proud to be me" (Fire)
Capricorn (The Goat) = Conformist "Your way is fine" (Earth)
Aquarius (Water Bearer) = Unconventional "Ideally …" (Air)
Pisces (The Fish) = Self-sacrificing "Whatever it takes" (Water)
Here's another way of looking at these eight signs:
Leo = I create (I did good! I am the greatest!)
Virgo = I perfect (We'll get this right eventually)
Libra = I balance (Let's all be friends)
Scorpio = I regenerate (I can make this work again)
Sagittarius = I aspire (There is no end to the possibilities)
Capricorn = I order (This goes here and that goes there)
Aquarius = I reform (You should do it this way)
Pisces = I redeem (Things are getting better)

These are a few ways of looking at the astrological signs. My suggestion to you is to find your own key words, phrases, or concepts for each of the twelve signs. If you don't have access to an astrology book try your local library. If you're looking for one reference book on the subject you might consider Thorsons's *Principles of Astrology* by Charles and Suzi Harvey which is a well-used reference book in my own library.

### 3

The twelve signs describe our personality. The ten planets are ten different aspects of our personality. A planet in a sign is one way to explain how that part of our personality behaves. Isn't this fun?

Here's one way to look at which part of our personality each of the planets explains:

Moon – Our subconscious mind, how we remember
Mercury – Our communications, how we speak and write
Venus – Our emotional mind, how we love
Sun – Our conscious mind, how we think
Mars – Our anger, how we assert ourselves
Jupiter – Our searching mind, how we expand ourselves
Saturn – Our fear, how we limit ourselves
Uranus – Our originality, how we change ourselves
Neptune – Our initiative, how we start new things
Pluto – Our regenerative ability, how we start over

This is only one way of defining the planets. There are dozens and dozens of other ways. As you grow and learn, you'll probably want to define the planets and the signs in your own words using your own knowledge base and personal experience. Good. Go for it. You'll find it to be an educational journey of inestimable value in your life.

Now you have twelve signs and ten planets and that's twenty-two things. Not surprisingly, there are also twenty-two trumps or keys in the Major Arcana. Any time you have twenty-two of this and twenty-two of that you can match them up one on one.

That's what we're going to do next, match the twenty-two keys of the tarot to the ten planets and twelve signs. If you want to have some fun, play with that concept for a while and in the next lesson you'll learn one way to do just that. But maybe by then you'll have come up with your own system for doing it.

## 4

We have just promised ourselves to match up the twelve signs of the zodiac and the ten planets with the twenty-two keys of the Major Arcana. Here's one way:

0 = Air (Uranus)
I = Mercury
II = Moon
III = Venus
IV = Aries
V = Taurus
VI = Gemini
VII = Cancer
VIII = Leo
IX = Virgo
X = Jupiter
XI = Libra
XII = Water (Neptune)
XIII = Scorpio
XIV = Sagittarius
XV = Capricorn
XVI = Mars
XVII = Aquarius

XVIII = Pisces
XIX = Sun
XX = Fire (Pluto)
XXI = Saturn

This is the method adopted by most of the Golden Dawn Orders though there are a few variations. Here's another system taught by Clifford Bias in his wonderful book *Qabalah, Tarot & the Western Mystery Tradition*:

0 = Air (Uranus)
I = Water (Neptune)
II = Fire (Pluto)
III = Saturn
IV = Leo
V = Taurus
VI = Cancer
VII = Scorpio
VIII = Libra
IX = Jupiter
X = Virgo
XI = Mars
XII = Gemini
XIII = Venus
XIV = Sun
XV = Mercury
XVI = Sagittarius
XVII = Aries
XVIII = Pisces
XIX = Capricorn
XX = Aquarius
XXI = Moon

One other interesting system is to assign the first ten cards to the ten planets in order and the next twelve cards to the twelve signs in order. That's not one of my personal favorites but some tarot readers feel quite comfortable using this system. There are several other systems. The one which works best for you is the one to choose to use. If that means you need to build your own system, so be it. Enjoy building! Match the cards up with the planets and signs any way you want. Then use it and make it work for you. It will.

To have fun with what you know so far try using only the Major Arcana and draw some cards for any question you want to use. See what the answers are from an astrological point of view. Here's one for the question: "Is the pace of this material just right? Too slow? Or too fast?"

Card 1 – The Fool (Uranus—How I change) = Just right
Card 2 – The Hermit (Virgo—I perfect and I serve) = Too slow
Card 3 – The Moon (Pisces—I redeem) = too fast

This material is being presented just right for me because this is "how I change" things in my life, at this pace. The material that's being presented too slowly for some feels that way because this is the pace at which "I serve" other people. So fill in the blanks yourself and expand your learning curve. The material that's coming too fast for some is a call for asking questions because "I will redeem" myself by helping you learn this in spite of everything. That was fun! Try your own fun next.

# 5

You have all the basics now except for the court cards. The planets are assigned to the ten ranks of the pip cards and to ten of the Major Arcana. The signs, or the planets that rule them, are assigned to the other twelve Major Arcana. You've got some meanings assigned to the four elements, the ten planets, and the twelve signs.

Congratulations! You're halfway there. The rest is easy!

In astrology we like to talk about the angles between planets and we call these aspects. Aspects are angles between planets. Some aspects are favorable and lucky. Some are not. The most important aspects are:

Sextile – an angle of 60 degrees
Square – an angle of 90 degrees
Trine – an angle of 120 degrees
Opposition – an angle of 180 degrees
Conjunction – an angle of zero degrees

As you might guess, oppositions are related to being the opposite; and an angle of 180 degrees is often said to be 180 degrees out of phase.

You can't get much more negative than that. So oppositions are said to be negative or unfavorable or just plain bad luck.

Squares are not quite as bad. In fact a square is just half an opposition so it's only half as bad. You might consider it as a little bit negative or tough luck.

Trines are considered to be very beneficial, very good luck, and positive energy. So trines are just the opposite of oppositions. Since three is a very lucky number and it takes three trines to make a circle, trines are very lucky.

Sextiles are half of a trine. So sextiles are lucky too but not as lucky as a trine. You might consider them slightly positive or a little lucky.

Can you guess what court cards we could assign to each of these aspects? Correct! We could assign any court card to any aspect and have a workable system for us. Here's my way, remembering that my way works for me but it may not work for you:

Pages = Sextiles
Knights = Squares
Queens = Trines
Kings = Oppositions

So what happens when you pull two court cards? How can you have a trine opposition, for example? Well, you can't. So one possibility is to say every time you pull two or more court cards what you have is a conjunction. That works for me, but what's a conjunction?

A conjunction happens when two planets are very close together in the same part of the heavens astrologically. Conjunctions mean whatever you want them to mean. One meaning is the planets are helping each other. Another is good planets help each other and negative planets make things harder for each other. But then you have to define the "good" planets. And the "negative planets."

One way to do that is to say the sun, Venus, and Jupiter are "good" and the moon, Mars, and Saturn are "bad." You can make the other four planets neutral or divide them up as Mercury and Neptune are good but Pluto and Uranus are bad. Or Uranus and Mercury are good. Or …

You get the picture. You get to decide how you want to define everything and make up your own system. But here's how the system we're discussing works:

Say you draw a Queen. That's a trine. That's very good luck, very favorable for the planets in the reading. That means you read the other cards in a very positive way. Say you draw a Knight. Oops. Things are a little negative and you read the cards accordingly. That's all there is to it. Now you have all the basics: planets, signs, aspects, and elements. And you've assigned these things to the pip cards, court cards, and Major Arcana. So what's left to do? Spreads. We'll do that in the final section of this chapter.

## 6

The horoscope is divided into twelve "houses." Each house is concerned with some part of our life. Different authors use slightly different names and descriptions for the houses. Here's a system developed for tarot readers:

| HOUSE | MEANING |
|---|---|
| 1. | My health |
| 2. | My money |
| 3. | My communications |
| 4. | My family |
| 5. | My relationships |
| 6. | My service to others |
| 7. | My attitude toward other people |
| 8. | My attitude toward other people's money |
| 9. | My attitude toward other people's ideas |
| 10. | My relatives |
| 11. | My career and business |
| 12. | My spiritual work |

Pick a house, draw a card, write down the meaning of the house and the name and meaning of the card. Interpret the meaning of the card as it relates to the meaning of the house. You just did a one-card reading. Wasn't that fun?

Pick two houses, draw two cards, write down the meanings of the houses and the name and meaning of the cards. Interpret the meanings of the cards as they relate to the meanings of the houses and you've done a two-card reading.

Pick up to twelve houses and choose a card for each house. Follow the same system and you've done a tarot reading based on the art and science of astrology. Practice this using all the information shared with you so far.

# CHAPTER 7

# Tarot dignities

1

The terms dignity and dignities refer to how cards placed next to a given card affect the meaning of that card. Dignity is the relationship between two or more cards. Dignities may be neutral, positive, or negative. This quality of neutral, positive, or negative is determined by the system or type of dignities the reader uses.

We'll discuss several systems of determining dignity. Elemental Dignity is determined by the element of the cards. Astrological Dignity is determined by the planet assigned to the cards. Numerological Dignity is determined by the relationship of the numbers assigned to the cards. Sequential Dignity is determined by the relationship of the cards to a sequence of numbers. Royal Dignity provides an interesting way of handling court cards in a reading.

First, let's define what we mean by the qualities of neutral, positive, and negative. For our purposes, neutral means the card in question is not affected by the cards around it. The total effect of all those cards is no effect. The card in question is read using its normal interpretation. A positive quality means the card in question is to be interpreted in a positive light. Negative quality means the card in question is to be interpreted in a negative light.

Let's say the card we're evaluating is the Ten of Swords which means "intellectually drained." If the Ten of Swords is neutrally dignified, this meaning doesn't change. If negatively dignified, it indicates an intellectual disaster. If positive, it may only be a temporary situation where the client is intellectually drained but will recover soon.

This is just an example. Rather than telling you what positive and negative dignity mean for each card, my intention is to give you a set of rules so you may define the cards the way you want to define them. Using dignities is a way of giving three meanings to each card. The neutral meaning is the meaning you've decided to give the card in question. Using this definition as your usual meaning for the card in question, come up with a positive and negative meaning for the same card.

Let's say the card you're evaluating is the Six of Cups which means happiness. If this card is negatively dignified, it could mean sadness or it could mean neither happy nor sad, neutral. If positive it might mean joy beyond description or very happy. There's a whole range of possible meanings. Each tarot reader needs to decide in advance which meanings he or she will use for neutral, positive, and negative dignities. Answer the question: How much positive, how much negative?

Some tarot readers use dignities instead of using reversed cards for this reason. Instead of two possible meanings, the reader has three possible interpretations any time two or more cards are used for a reading. In my own systems, I normally use both reversals and dignities with my three-, five-, ten-, and twelve-card spreads. This gives me six possible meanings for each card. When using one-card draws, using dignities isn't an option.

My suggestion is for you to learn to use one form of dignity or reversals first and add more systems later. My second suggestion is to always use the same system with the same deck. This suggestion is to have a different deck for each system and not use the same deck with more than one system. The rest of the suggestion is to learn one system at a time. This is the second thing we needed to discuss.

To use dignities you need to define each card three ways: neutral, positive, or negative. Or, you need to devise a set of rules for knowing how positively and how negatively those dignities will affect each card. You can do this before or after you've decided what system of dignities you're going to use.

Your homework, should you choose to try dignities, is to choose a deck for the system you're going to build and define each card with three meanings as described. In the next section we'll define numerological dignities.

## 2

If you've been studying and working with your cards as suggested in the last section, you now have three key words, phrases, or concepts for each of your tarot cards. One of these meanings is the normal meaning you attribute to each card. The second meaning is more positive and the third more negative. That's a good start.

The next step is to decide when dignities come into play. Let's assume dignities come into play whenever two cards are next to each other in any direction. There are no cards between the two cards in question. With a three-card spread where the cards are laid out in a row, the dignity of the middle card is affected by the other two cards. The dignity of the two end cards is affected only by the middle card. But if three cards are laid out in a triangle, then the dignity of each card is affected by the other two.

With a five-card spread laid out in a row, the dignity of the two end cards is affected only by the card next to them. The dignity of the middle three cards is affected by the cards lying on either side of them. But if the same five cards are laid out in a cross, the dignity of the middle card is affected by all four of the other cards. The dignity of the four cards forming the cross is affected by the middle card and the two cards on either side of the card in question.

Sounds complicated, but it isn't. If one card is positive and the other negative, the result is no effect or neutral. If two cards are positive or negative, you can read this as either very positive or negative or just positive or negative.

This is a decision you make when you're building your system. Here's a seemingly complicated system to show you how it works. This system is a Spirit-Mind-Emotions-Intuition-Body spread with Spirit in the middle, Air above, Water on the left, Fire on the right, and Earth below. Each card is defined with the neutral meaning. This doesn't mean the definition of the card is neutral. It defines what the card means when the card's dignity is neutral.

Then an extremely positive and an extremely negative definition are given to each card. This is the best-case/worst-case scenario and represents the best possible and worst possible meaning of the card. The best possible positive meaning is used when the subject card is in the middle of a five-card spread and the other four cards are all in positive dignity to it. The worst possible meaning is used when the other four cards are all adversely (negatively) dignified to the central card.

Now's a good time to talk about how tarot readers refer to positive and negative dignities. Positive dignity is also called beneficial, helpful, good luck, and fortunate dignity. Negative dignity is also called adverse, inimical, bad luck, troublesome, and ill-dignified. What you call positive and negative dignities is entirely up to you.

Next, define a positive meaning in the middle between neutral and extremely positive, and a negative meaning in the middle between neutral and extremely negative. This meaning is used when the net result of the dignity is plus or minus two. Plus two means there's a net of two positive dignities and minus two means there's a net of two negative dignities. If three cards are positive and one is negative, the net is plus two. If two cards are negative and the third is neutral, the result is minus two. Positive and negative meanings are used when the net result is plus two or minus two respectively.

You now have five definitions for each card—extremely negative, negative, neutral, positive, and extremely positive. These five definitions will serve you well for all three-card tarot spreads. For five-card spreads you may want to add two more positive and two more negative meanings. These are slightly positive which is plus one and halfway between neutral and positive; and slightly negative which is minus one and halfway between neutral and negative. Then you also derive very positive which is plus three and halfway between positive and extremely positive; and very negative which is minus three and halfway between negative and extremely negative. You now have nine meanings for each card:

| | |
|---|---|
| Extremely positive | plus four |
| Very positive | plus three |
| Positive | plus two |
| Slightly positive | plus one |
| Neutral | |
| Slightly negative | minus one |
| Negative | minus two |
| Very negative | minus three |
| Extremely negative | minus four |

As you can see, it's not as complicated as it looks. For three-card spreads and other spreads where no more than two other cards affect the dignity, you only need five meanings for each card:

| | |
|---|---|
| Positive | plus two |
| Slightly positive | plus one |
| Neutral | |
| Slightly negative | minus one |
| Negative | minus two |

Numerology, as I mentioned in an earlier chapter, reduces every number greater than nine to a single-digit number by adding together the digits in the number. The result is always a number greater than zero and less than ten. For example, the number ten is a double-digit number, so we add the digits one and zero to obtain the number one. Thus, ten reduces to one. Fourteen reduces to five. Twenty-one reduces to three. Nineteen reduces to ten and then to one. The final result is always a single-digit number and it's called the Root Number.

When using numerology with tarot cards, the court cards are numbered sequentially 11–14. In the standard Rider-Waite Tarot the Pages are eleven, Knights are twelve, Queens thirteen, and Kings fourteen. The numbers of the tarot trumps are the number assigned to each Key. You'll need to decide how to number any cards which are not numbered in your deck.

It is this root number we use to determine the dignity between any two cards. The rules for determining dignity are based on the relationship of the numbers to each other. The odd numbers 1–3–5–7–9 are positively influenced by other odd numbers. All even numbers 0–2–4–6–8 are positively influenced by other even numbers. The odd numbers 1–3–5–7 are negatively influenced by any even number 2–4–6–8 and neutral to the number zero. The even numbers 2–4–6–8 are negatively influenced by any odd number 1–3–5–7 and neutral to the number nine. Nine is helpful to other odd numbers and has no effect on even numbers. Zero is helpful to other even numbers and has no effect on the odd numbers.

Here's a summary of the rules for determining Numerological Dignity:

1. Even root numbers are positively dignified to other even numbers
2. Odd root numbers are positively dignified to other odd numbers

3. The even root numbers 2–3–4–8 are negatively dignified to the odd numbers
4. The odd root numbers 1–3–5–7 are negatively dignified to the even numbers
5. The number zero is neutral to all odd numbers
6. The number nine is neutral to all even numbers

We'll do some example readings in the next section using this system. Your assignment, if you decide to play with Numerological Dignities, is to play with them.

## 3

The example readings in this section are done using the Numerological Dignities explained in the past two lessons. These examples are created for instructional purposes only, and any similarity to a real tarot reading is purely coincidental.

Q – What outcome can I expect from creating the Temple Amulet in a ritual this evening?
A – A five-card Elemental Cross spread was used.
    Earth (above) = Knight of Disks (12 = 3)
    Water (left) = Ten of Cups (10 = 1)
    Spirit (center) = The Devil (15 = 6)
    Air (right) = Five of Swords (5)
    Fire (below) = Knight of Wands (12 = 3)

Every card is an odd root number except the middle card. So each of the four directional cards have two positive and one negative dignity for a total of +1 meaning slightly more positive than the normal meaning. But the middle card, the Spirit card has four negative dignities. This total of -4 means gives a very negative meaning to this card.

Since amulets are basic spiritual tools, this does not appear to be a good time to create a Temple Amulet unless we want that temple to be really tied down in the mundane world. It doesn't matter how positive the rest of the reading is. Very negative is warning enough.

Q – What's the probable outcome of running a new advertisement for the Institute?

A – A three-card Mind-Emotions-Spirit spread was used (this is an Air-Water-Spirit spread).
Air = Ace of Disks (1) (New venture)
Water = Five of Swords (5) (Conflict)
Spirit = Ten of Wands (10 = 1) (Heavy burden)

The two end cards are +1 and the middle card +2 (positive) in this reading. The reading is: The venture started off well and is now facing a minor conflict of ideas regarding running a new advertisement. Notice how the +2 changes the Five of Swords from a very negative card to a fairly neutral card. The outcome is going to be a mixed bag but overall it's a positive burden. To me a positive burden is doing something you love to do but it's a lot of work.

Q – How well will the cat recover?
A – The spread is a three-card triangle spread for Past-Present-Future.
Past = Princess of Swords (11 = 2) (fairness)
Present = Six of Swords (6) (harmony)
Future = Nine of Cups (9) (happiness)

On the surface it looks like the Nine of Cups has a negative influence on the other two cards, but by definition the nines are neutral. Therefore the Nine of Cups is +2 while the other two are each +1 or slightly positive. The overall picture is positive. The past and present cards indicate the illness isn't serious and the Nine of Cups promises a lasting cure.

Q – What's the probable outcome of doing the candle ritual tonight?
A – Using a three-card Past-Present-Future spread laid out in a line, we have:
Past = Princess of Cups (11 = 2) (Loving friend)
Present = Seven of Cups (7) (Illusion)
Future = Key XX (20 = 2) (Spiritual rebirth)

The two end cards are negatively dignified and the middle card is (–2) very negatively dignified. The candle ritual won't have a positive result if performed tonight. I'd really be fooling myself to believe otherwise (very negative Seven of Cups). Both the foundation for this ritual and the future outcome are negative. The loving friend may not support the ritual or may withdraw and any rebirth will have negative consequences.

Without using Numerological Dignities with this reading there's nothing to indicate this ritual would have bad consequences. On the other hand, using Elemental Dignities (to be discussed later) a very positive outcome could be expected.

You're probably wondering how the same cards can give such opposite recommendations. The secret is in the system of dignities you choose to use. Which system you use is really immaterial. They all work. Try them all and see what works best for you. Use that system.

One more reading, and this time the Numerological Dignity system provides a more positive result than most other dignity systems would.

Q – What can we expect if we change servers?
A – Using the five-card Elemental Cross spread:
    Earth (above) – Five of Wands (5) – Conflict
    Water (left) – Seven of Cups (7) – Illusion
    Spirit (center) – Ten of Swords (10 = 1) – Ruin
    Air (right) – Tower (16 = 7) – Awakening
    Fire (below) – Five of Pentacles (5) – Loss of Money

Our first impression might not be very positive if we just look at these cards and remember what they mean to us. Any one of them by itself sends a rather negative message. But here, every card has as odd-numbered root.

Earth and Fire are each +2. Air, Water, and Spirit are all +3. Looked at in this manner, this reading becomes pretty positive. Conflict becomes a minor irritation, a no-never-mind. Illusion becomes reality, Ruin becomes a good idea, and loss of money becomes a minor overhead expense. The Awakening is a very positive one. Changing servers is going to be a good thing to do.

Your assignment, should you choose to experiment with Numerological Dignities, is to do a few spreads and see how you like the system. In the next section we'll discuss a few variations that might be of interest.

## 4

There are several optional way of looking at numerological dignities. Here we'll consider a few of them.

If you don't like defining both zero and nine as neutral, you can just leave them alone. Zero would be an even number and the nines would be odd. You don't need to make any other changes.

If you prefer to define the Major Arcana as always being neutral, you also have that option. Neutral cards have no effect on the cards around them. You have the option of allowing other cards to affect the trump Key or not. For example, suppose your three-card spread is:

Past = (left) Queen of Wands (13 = 4)
Present = (center) Hierophant (5)
Future = (right) Two of Swords (2)

You need to decide in advance if the Hierophant will be adversely affected twice by the two even numbers or not. The Queen and Two are considered neutral because of the trump beside them. The Hierophant can be interpreted as being neutrally affected or negatively affected twice according to how you set down your rules.

The normal rules are: Odd numbers enhance other odd numbers; even numbers enhance other even numbers; even and odd numbers conflict with each other negatively; Major Arcana have no effect on the other cards in the spread. If you want, you can add that no cards have any effect on the Major Arcana.

Rather than going through the process of calculating the Root Numbers (19 = 10 = 1, for example), you can just use even numbers vs. odd numbers. So the card twenty-one would be odd "on sight" instead of going through the process of finding the Root Number (21 = 3 which is also odd). This will cause a few problems if you don't let your subconscious mind in on the new rules. Key XI for example would be odd whereas the root of eleven is the even number two. In fact, all of the numbers from ten through nineteen will have a different polarity using this approach. The rules are the same: Odd numbers enhance odd numbers, even numbers enhance even numbers, and the conflict between even and odd numbers is negative. Trump cards can be considered neutral when using this system but that's not a requirement.

# 5

Astrological dignities are based on the affinities and antipathies certain planets have for each other. The usual grouping of planets when using astrological dignities is:

Masculine: Mars, Uranus, and Pluto
Feminine: Venus, Neptune, and Saturn
Neutral: Mercury, Jupiter, sun, and moon

This may not be the assignment you prefer, so you're encouraged to start right out by creating your own system. Decide which polarities you want to use (masculine, feminine, neutral) and which planets you want to assign to each of these polarities. Either way, step one in creating a system for using astrological dignities is to use the suggested system of polarities or create your own.

The basic rules are very simple:

- Masculine planets are positive towards other masculine planets
- Feminine planets are positive towards other feminine planets
- Neutral planets have no effect on the other planets
- Masculine and feminine planets are negative towards each other
- Other planets see the sun and Mercury as masculine
- Other planets see the moon and Jupiter as feminine

Again, if you don't like these rules, write your own. To do this you'll need to decide how many neutral cards you want then divide the rest of the deck up into two parts: masculine and feminine. That's all there is to it. Make up your own rules and you've finished the second step in creating your own system for using astrological dignities. Otherwise, step two is to learn the basic rules.

The third step is to assign the planets to the cards. For astrological dignities we normally use only the planets and not the signs. You can use the ruling planet of each sign if you decide to use signs too. Or you could use the signs as well as the planets. This requires you to decide the polarity of the signs. My impulse is to make the Fire and Air signs masculine and the Water and Earth signs feminine. But that's just my opinion. This is your system, build it the way you want to build it. You'll find that's easier and it works better for you anyway.

## 6

We'll continue building a system for using astrological dignities started in the last section. The next step in the process of building a system for using astrological dignities is to assign the planets to the cards.

One easy way to do that with the pip cards is to assign them in order, like this: Neptune, Uranus, Saturn, Jupiter, Mars, sun, Venus, Mercury, moon, Pluto.

The system used for assigning the planets to the Major Arcana can be done in the same manner. The usual method in use today is that developed by the Hermetic Order of the Golden Dawn. That's the system used by the Rider-Waite-Smith tarot deck and most decks of that genre. You're encouraged to develop your own correspondences between the planets and the signs. Here's the one used by the Golden Dawn:

Zero – Uranus
  1 – Mercury
  2 – Moon
  3 – Venus
  4 – Aries (Mars)
  5 – Taurus (Venus)
  6 – Gemini (Mercury)
  7 – Cancer (Moon)
  8 – Leo (Sun)
  9 – Virgo (Mercury)
10 – Jupiter
11 – Libra (Venus)
12 – Neptune
13 – Scorpio (Pluto)
14 – Sagittarius (Jupiter)
15 – Capricorn (Saturn)
16 – Mars
17 – Aquarius (Uranus)
18 – Pisces (Neptune)
19 – Sun
20 – Pluto
21 – Saturn

The court cards present an interesting problem. There are ten planets and sixteen cards. Some planets will need to be used more than once if the planets are assigned to these sixteen cards. One option is to use the court cards as always being neutral so no planetary assignment needs to be made. Another option is to assign the Pages and Queens to the feminine polarity and the Kings and Knights to the masculine. A third option is to use the polarities for determining how other cards impact the court cards but consider the court cards neutral for evaluating the cards around them.

You can also assign four planets to the four ranks of court cards just like the Minor Arcana. For example:

Pages = Saturn
Knights = Uranus
Queens = Neptune
Kings = Pluto

This is the approach we're going to use in building this system for using astrological dignities. It's an interesting system worthy of your consideration. Other planetary assignments are also workable. With both the pip cards and the court cards you have four cards of each rank. You can handle these by assigning specific meanings to the suits or to the elements. There are a lot of options but that gives you a lot to work with as you build your own system for astrological dignities. Your assignment, should you elect to participate, is to experiment with this system, or the system you create, or any other system of your choice.

## 7

We're going to do some readings now using the astrological dignities propounded in the last few sections. Since the important thing here is applying the dignities, I won't complete the readings. Consider trying to complete them yourself so you can get more practice interpreting the cards.

Q – Where will I find true love?
A – Using a three-card triangle spread:
    Mind = 3 Cups (Saturn = F)
    Body = 6 Coins (Sun = N)
    Heart = Knight of Wands (Uranus = M)

The Mind card is positively influenced and means more and better whatever it is. The Body card is completely neutral and has its original meaning. The Heart card is negatively influenced and means less than it otherwise would.

Q – When will I find a new job?
A – Using a five-card star spread:
    Air (E) – 7 Wands (Venus = F)
    Fire (S) – Hermit (Mercury = N)
    Water (W) – 2 Swords (Uranus = M)
    Earth (N) – Key XX (Pluto = M)
    Spirit (C) – 10 Wands (Pluto = M)

Air is plus 2 (2M and 1N), Fire is plus 1 (2M and 1F), Water is plus 2 (2M and 1N), Earth is plus 1 (2M and 1F), Spirit is plus 1 (2M, 1F, and 1N).

Q – Why do I feel depressed?
A – Using a five-card star spread:
    Air = Strength (Sun = N)
    Fire = 7 Swords (Venus = F)
    Water = Page of Cups (Saturn = F)
    Earth = Devil (Saturn = F)
    Spirit = 5 Wands (Mars = M)

Air is minus 1 (2F and 1M), Fire is neutral (F + M + N), Water is minus 1 (2F and 1M), Earth is neutral (M + F + N), Spirit is minus 3 (3F and 1 N).

As with astrological systems for reading tarot cards, the secret for using astrological dignities is to decide which cards are positive, which are negative, and which are neutral in your system. One of my students has a very simple system you might like to consider. The sun, Mercury, Venus, and the moon are all positive (inside Earth's orbit). Mars, Saturn, Jupiter, and Uranus are negative (outside Earth's orbit). Neptune and Pluto are neutral because they're too far away and besides, they may be mother and child (planet and lost moon).

Whatever you decide is what's important. Your subconscious and intuitive minds will both accept your definitions and use those definitions to communicate with you in the symbols you have available for them. Whatever system you use is exactly the system they'll use to communicate with you.

That's why it's so difficult to answer a question like: "What's the Four of Wands mean in this reading?" The answer is the Four of Wands means exactly what the reader defined it to be. If the reader defined Wands to be intuitive insights and four to be Jupiter. The answer is "Jupiter Intuitive Insights." Now all you have to know is how the reader defined Jupiter. If Jupiter is Good Luck, the answer to the reader's question is good luck through intuitive insights.

## 8

The most commonly used form of dignities is elemental dignities. The rules for this system are very simple though you can complicate them as much as you desire:

Rule 1 – Wands and Swords are masculine
Rule 2 – Cups and Coins are feminine
Rule 3 – Major Arcana are always neutral
Rule 4 – Masculine are negative to feminine
Rule 5 – Masculine are positive to masculine
Rule 6 – Feminine are positive to feminine
Rule 7 – Feminine are negative to masculine

When using one-card draws, first decide which element best matches the question. Then apply the above rules to that element instead of a second card.

Here's a few examples using this system of dignities:

Q – Will I get the raise I'm expecting?
A – Using a five-card star spread:
    Air = Chariot (N)
    Fire = Wheel of Fortune (N)
    Water = King of Cups (F)
    Earth = Three of Cups (F)
    Spirit = Six of Coins (F)

The Chariot and the Wheel are both neutral and the other cards have no effect on them using the given rules. The King of Cups and the Three of Cups are both plus two because they have one neutral and two feminine cards touching them. The Six of Coins is plus two because two feminine cards touch it. So the answer is "yes" by a vote of three to none with two abstaining votes.

Q – Does this system work?
A – Using a triangle spread: For-Against—Answer, the cards drawn were the Six of Cups, the Seven of Swords, and the Emperor which

is neutral. The dignity of the last card, the answer card is neutral. This means both yes and no or in other words, maybe. The full answer is this system works if this is the system you select. It doesn't work otherwise.

Q – Will my husband return from Iraq soon?

A – Using the same triangle spread the cards drawn for this reading were the Nine of Wands, Two of Swords, and Seven of Wands. Since all these cards are masculine the Seven of Wands is to be interpreted as very positive (+2) and the answer is a resounding yes. (Her husband retuned two weeks later and has been re-stationed locally.)

This is all there really is to elemental dignities. You can redefine them any way you like and develop your own system.

Here's a different approach using the Dynamic Elemental Spreads discussed in an earlier chapter. Use the above rules but apply them based on the position of the card and not on the other cards in the spread. Assign the element of Spirit to be neutral as well as the Major Arcana which represent Spirit. For example, let's redo the first question, "Will I get the raise I'm expecting?" The cards drawn were:

Air = Chariot (Neutral to Air)
Fire = Wheel of Fortune (Neutral to Air)
Water = King of Cups (Positive to Water)
Earth = Three of Cups (Positive to Earth)
Spirit = Six of Coins (Neutral to Spirit)

The answer is still yes (two positive and three neutral) but it's not quite as strong as the first reading. Now there are three abstaining votes.

You can use this on a Body-Mind-Spirit (Earth, Air, Spirit) spread just as easily. Let's use the second question and place the cards in this format: Earth = Six of Cups (+), Air = Seven of Swords (+), and Spirit = Emperor (N). If Spirit were positive to Spirit, this would be a completely positive answer. Since two pluses outweigh one neutral, the final answer by the preponderance of evidence is positive.

## 9

The technique of applying the dignity of the card to the position of that card in the spread can be used with just about any tarot spread you want. All you need to do is assign an element to each position in the spread. Then decide what rules you want to enforce for elemental dignities. Using this approach, I like to have the Major Arcana be neutral toward the masculine and feminine positions but positive toward Spiritual positions in the tarot spread. That's just my personal preference at this time. One neat thing about tarot reading is I get to choose how I do it, my personal preferences count.

Using court cards to determine dignity is a lot of fun. It works like this: An even number of court cards in a reading is positive and an odd number of court cards in a reading is negative. If there are no court cards, that's neutral. You can use this method and give a regular meaning to the court cards. You can also use this method and give no other meaning to the court cards except to determine dignity. I call this technique Court Card Dignities.

You know, for beginning students really having a problem with court cards, this isn't a bad approach. It gives your subconscious mind sixteen cards to play with to help you determine dignity. You can even say having three court cards is more negative than just one court card; and five court cards in a reading is even more negative. You can say that four, six, or any higher even number of court cards in a reading becomes more and more positive.

Another way of using court cards for dignities is to say the card in front of a court card (the card that the figure in the court card is facing) is positively influenced and the card behind the court card is negatively influenced. You can use this same rule for the Major Arcana or for the Minor Arcana or both. Cards facing ahead could be used as favorable for cards beneath them or they could just be considered neutral. If you decide to use forward-facing cards as positive to the card below, then backward-facing cards would be positive to cards above.

You can have a lot of fun using this technique for court cards, pip cards, or Major Arcana. You can even have fun naming these techniques. I call these techniques Court Facing Dignities, Pip Facing Dignities, and Trump Facing Dignities. You can use any combination of them. My personal favorite is Court and Trump Facing Dignities and I assign meanings to the courts.

Another form of dignity you might enjoy trying is called Trump Dignities. The rules for this technique are very simple. Any upright trump card is a positive influence on all other cards in the spread. Any inverted trump is a negative influence on all other cards in the spread. You have the option to allow trumps to be neutral to each other, but the system is designed so all trump cards have an influence on all other cards in the spread—even other trump cards.

Using this approach, you can read all the cards in the spread as though they were upright. This means you only need to memorize one key word, phrase, or concept for each card. Then you apply the dignities according to the direction of the Major Arcana cards and make that memorized meaning either more positive or more negative according to the direction of the trumps. One other rule to remember is a positive and a negative result in no change of meaning for the card being considered.

You can expand trump dignities by using all cards in the deck. This is called Inverted Dignities and the rules are the same but apply to all cards and not just the trumps. Let's say you select five cards, three are upright and two are inverted. The net result is plus one. So all cards are read with a slightly positive meaning. Four upright cards out of five would be very positive and all five upright would be extremely positive using this approach. Again, no other meaning needs to be given to the cards. Each card can have one meaning and the meaning is not modified if the card in inverted. It is, however, modified by the other cards around it.

In my opinion, this is a good approach for people who have a hard time memorizing the meanings of the cards. If you have a really hard time, you can use a deck with printed meanings and modify those meanings up or down depending upon the inverted dignities. I use this system myself with the Thoth deck. I never got interested in memorizing the inverted meanings of the cards in the deck. I like the names given the cards already. It just seemed natural to me to use inverted dignities with this deck. I do.

There's one variation of Elemental Dignities that appeals to me but I don't use it very often. The idea is to classify the question by element. Then all the cards of that element in the spread are more positive than cards of the other elements. You can even use cards of the same energy (masculine or feminine) as being more positive than others in the spread.

How I use this concept is not for dignities but for identifying more important cards in the spread. For questions about money, it seems to me Earth cards are more important in the reading. For readings about careers, Fire cards are more important. Water cards would be more important for relationship questions and Air for questions about thoughts and ideas.

This finishes my discussion of tarot dignities. I hope you find something that appeals to you, something you can use, change, modify, and make a part of your tarot skills.

CHAPTER 8

# How to develop your intuition

## 1

You are intuitive. You have an active intuitive mind. You can tune in to your intuitive mind any time you want. These incontrovertible truths are based on universal law. Everybody who can think is able to intuit. It's your birthright to be intuitive, or "psychic" as some people call it. It's natural to be intuitive. It's normal.

The truth is you really don't "develop" your intuition. You just recognize it for what it is. You develop your ability to recognize and understand your own intuitive insights. You develop your ability to differentiate between imagination and intuition. You distinguish or discriminate one from the other.

From ancient times, intuitive people have explained that their inner voice is a small, quiet voice. It speaks softly and quietly to us all the time. We don't hear it for several reasons:

- Our thinking mind is chattering away
- Our imagination is running wild
- Our memories are flooding us

- Our emotions are excited and energetic
- Our bodies demand something

Before we can hear our small, quiet intuitive voice, we need to quiet down all this interference. The first step is to quiet down the "body mind." This mind tells us what our body needs from us. It tells us things like:

- Drink that coffee, soda, water, or something
- Eat that chocolate, doughnut, cake, or something
- Scratch me here or there where the itch is
- Relieve this bladder as soon as possible
- Empty this intestine now before I do
- Rub these shoulders or aching muscle
- Move that leg, or hand, or toe, or something

The messages we receive from our "body mind" usually launch us into some activity to satisfy the needs, wants, and desires of the body. The body can be quite demanding. It is demanding. Prove it to yourself. Just sit quietly, close your eyes, and forget about everything else. Just be with your body. In almost no time you'll find yourself moving some body part, scratching this or that, relieving pressure here or there, doing something your body wants you to do.

Refuse to do it. Just sit there and observe how the body intensifies its demands. The pressure to move builds, the itches seem to multiply and grow stronger, tense muscles start to get harder and more painful. The body is speaking. It demands your attention.

This is happening to you all day, every day whether you're aware of it or not. We habitually answer the demands of our body. We move. We scratch. We tense and release muscles. We do this without thinking. We do it automatically. Habitually.

Your first step in tuning in to your own intuitive mind is to quiet down the body mind (also called the animal mind, the unconscious, the primitive mind). You do this by relaxing the body and breathing deeply and rhythmically. If you're not accustomed to completely relaxing your body, you might like to try a couple of exercises that have proven helpful to generations of students.

The first is a simple contraction-relaxation exercise. It goes like this:

Get into a comfortable sitting or reclining position. Adjust your position until you're quite comfortable. Concentrate on your left foot.

Tighten the muscles in your left foot slowly until they're intensely rigid. Hold this muscle-contracted position for a couple of seconds and then let go. Completely relax your left foot. Let go of all tension.

Repeat this exercise for your right foot, then your left calf, right calf, and work your way up your body from feet to head: feet, calves, thighs, hips, lower abdomen, lower back, stomach, middle back, chest, upper back, hands, forearms, upper arms, shoulders, neck, and face. In the beginning this exercise can take twenty to thirty minutes to completely relax your body. The benefits of this exercise are to release toxins from your muscles, improve blood flow and oxygenation to your muscles and organs, and to release tension.

Over a few days of practice you can go through this whole sequence in less than five minutes. You will be able to relax every muscle completely in just a few minutes. Over a few weeks of practice you can do this whole sequence in less than a minute. Over a few months you can do it in a few seconds.

The second exercise is deep breathing (also called abdominal breathing and yogic breathing). While in a relaxed state, force all of the air out of your lungs and hold it for a second. Then allow your abdomen to inflate while your chest remains compressed. Let the air flow in and out without effort as you raise and relax your abdomen. This is the first phase of abdominal deep breathing.

After a few breaths, allow your chest to inflate after your lower lungs are filled with air. Hold your breath for a second. Relax and let the air from your chest expel first. Then pull in your abdomen and let the rest of the air in your lungs move out. Pause and repeat. This is the second phase of deep breathing.

One caution: Never force your breath. Always be relaxed and comfortable before you start deep breathing, while deep breathing, and after you're done with the exercise.

As you quiet down and relax your body, abdominal breathing becomes easier. My suggestion is to do only the first exercise until you can completely relax your whole body in less than five minutes. Then add the second exercise. First get relaxed and then breathe deeply. The benefits of deep breathing are more energy, deeper relaxation, removal of toxins from the lungs, calmer state of mind, and greater emotional control.

It may seem strange to you to relax and breathe as a first step toward opening your intuitive mind. But thousands of teachers have been teaching this technique for thousands of years with good results.

Students who take this first step discover things about themselves they never knew. They become calmer and more peaceful, less anxious and less depressed, more energetic and more intuitive. Try it and see what you experience.

## 2

Once you've learned to completely relax your body and dismiss its incessant demands, you're ready to quiet down your active mind. You relax your body by first finding a very comfortable position, then letting go all body tension of any kind. You breathe deeply (abdominal breathing) and relax every muscle.

As explained in the first section, the benefits of complete relaxation and deep breathing include more energy, deeper relaxation, removal of toxins from the body, calmer state of mind, and greater emotional control. With practice, you can completely relax and receive these benefits in only a few moments—definitely in less than a minute.

Once your body is completely relaxed and you're breathing deeply, your mind will become overactive. It's natural. That's why we call it the "active" mind. Your active mind is really three separate and distinct minds all working together or contrary to each other.

The first part of your active mind is your subconscious mind. Your subconscious mind is your memory of everything in your life. It's your past, or at least what you consciously and unconsciously remember of your past. When you start thinking about things which have already occurred in your life (or in a past life), you're accessing your subconscious mind. Usually this is the first mind you access when you get very relaxed and comfortable.

Your subconscious mind is also your "good and faithful servant" which will do anything it can to serve you. When you ask for something in your life, your subconscious mind will do anything within its power to accomplish that request. Herein lies great untapped power. By simply asking your subconscious mind to stop remembering you can quiet it down. By asking it to help you tune in to your intuition, you get help. It's really that simple. Ask, and your subconscious mind will do everything within its power to do exactly what you ask. It really is your good and faithful servant.

When your subconscious mind quiets down and helps you access your intuitive mind, you'll usually start imagining all sorts of possibilities.

This is your second active mind, your imagination, at work. Your imagination imagines your future just as your subconscious remembers your past. Your imagination can be controlled as easily as your subconscious mind. Ask it to stop imagining the possibilities, and it will. Ask it to imagine you communicating directly with your intuitive mind, and it will help you do exactly that. You can easily shut out the past and the future by using this simple technique of redirecting your subconscious and imaginative minds to help you tune in to your intuition.

The third part of your active mind is your rational mind. This mind operates in the here and now. Your rational mind is your two-year-old-tantrum-throwing mind. It likes to do things its own way. It's your own personal critic. It also flatters you. Either way, it tries to control you. It is not your "good and faithful servant." It may be your own private demon. Your rational mind does not behave well when you ask it to stop thinking. It doesn't like to do what you ask it to do. It won't help you tune in to your intuition. In some ways your conscious mind is in competition with your intuitive mind.

There are several ways to calm down your thinking (rational) mind. One way is to occupy it with a saying of some kind. The yogis call this "mantra." It doesn't matter what you say. What matters is you just say it to yourself, inside your head, over and over. Occupy your mind with saying something over and over. If you're on a spiritual path, you may want to use the Divine name of your choice to occupy your mind.

You can use a yoga mantra like "Om Nama Shivaya" (pronounced om na ma she veye ya). You can use an affirmation like "I am, I can, I don't have to." Any affirmation will do. You can repeat the words to a poem or song or even an essay. Here's one of my favorites: "I am an intuitive person. My subconscious mind is helping me tune in to my intuition. My imaginative mind is helping me tune in to my intuition. My body is relaxed and sleeping. My rational mind is calm and listening alertly to the small quiet voice of my intuition." This is a long mantra or affirmation, but it says it all. Over and over it says it all.

Another way to quiet down your rational mind is to ignore it. Treat it like a child. Any time you become aware you're thinking, tell your mind you're not interested and dismiss it. Most rational minds don't like to be dismissed, so they keep coming back like a child with something else to talk about. If you're using this technique, keep saying you're not interested and dismiss it. Eventually your rational mind will go off somewhere and pout like the child that it is. That's all there is to it.

- Place your body in a comfortable position
- Completely relax your body and release all tension
- Breathe deeply
- Refocus your imaginative mind on tuning in to your intuition
- Ignore or occupy your rational mind
- Listen attentively for your intuitive mind

After just a few practice sessions, you'll hear that small, quiet voice that comes from deep within you and you'll know your intuition is alive and well.

## 3

If you've been experimenting with this system for developing your intuition, here's a synopsis of your experiences:

BODY MIND – Your body didn't want to settle down in the beginning. It told you to scratch this itch here or there, move this muscle or that, drink water or drain it, snack on something, or do something else. Your body is used to being in command and it likes being the boss.

As you practiced, your body tended to quiet down and relax more quickly, and willingly gave up the fight to be in control. The more you practiced the more your body relaxed and let go. This is normal so don't worry about it.

SUBCONSCIOUS MIND – As you started to quiet your mind down from the cares and woes of your life, your subconscious mind became active. You remembered to do this or that. You started thinking about your past, things you did or didn't do.

As you practiced telling your subconscious mind you didn't want to remember anything from your past just now and asked it to help you tune in to your intuitive mind, your subconscious mind complied.

Memories from your past faded away. You didn't know it, but as this happens your subconscious does go to work opening channels to your intuition. This is normal, so don't worry about it.

IMAGINATIVE MIND – As your subconscious mind stopped bringing up past memories, your imagination started running wild. You started thinking about all the possibilities of this or that. You took flights of fantasy and had a wonderfully exciting time.

As you practiced telling your imagination you didn't want to think about the possibilities just now and asked it to tune in to your intuitive mind, your imaginative mind complied. Future possibilities faded from your mind, not to be forgotten, but to be put on hold. Your imagination went to work helping you imagine yourself communicating with your own intuition. This is normal, so don't worry about it.

RATIONAL MIND – As your imagination stopped bringing up future possibilities, your thinking mind took over. This is probably when you started thinking you'd never become intuitive. Don't snicker. That's what we do to ourselves all the time. Nobody can criticize us as well as we can. When we temporarily stop remembering who and what we are, and when we temporarily stop fantasizing about whom and what we can become, we think we can't do it.

As you practiced ignoring your rational mind, you became calmer and more centered. I have an image of my rational mind becoming a small sulking boy hiding in the corner of my mind when I have reached this stage in my intuitive development. Others have different experiences but the end result is the same. We reach a point where our rational mind stops finding something wrong with us and it quiets down. This is normal, so don't worry about it.

WHAT'S NEXT: Practice is the next and most important step. It doesn't matter how long you practice in each session. What seems to matter most is regular practice. Two times a day is better than just once. Three times yields more results more quickly.

A few short sessions every day yields results more quickly than one long session a day. The process gets easier and easier with practice. Within a few weeks you will be able to completely relax your body and calm your mind. Now you know why we call your subconscious, imaginative, and rational minds the active mind.

# 4

If you've been practicing the techniques being discussed, you've probably already visited your intuitive mind. If not, why not review the previous lessons and give it a try? Here are the steps involved:

- Completely relax your body
- Breathe deeply
- Stop thinking about the past
- Enlist the help of your subconscious mind
- Stop thinking about future possibilities
- Enlist the help of your imagination
- Stop thinking about here and now
- Dismiss the thoughts that come to your mind
- Enter the peace and quiet of your mind

If only it were that easy in the beginning! If your mind works anything like mine, every practice session ended up with me writing a long To Do list. It's amazing how many things I'd forgotten to do and all the great ideas that popped into my mind. Some of them actually were quite good. Some of them were trash. Admittedly, most of them were not too good.

In other words, my memory and imagination got in the way. So did my personal critic, commonly known as my rational mind. But every once in a while my intuitive mind got through all this clatter and I really did have a good idea. The problem was I didn't know which was which and what was intuitive and what wasn't.

That's normal, so if it happens to you, please don't worry about it. Just cut to the chase. "Save the Best and Trash the Rest." Don't waste your time on a really bad idea.

It took me several weeks before I could recognize the difference between the "voices" of my different minds. Here's how it worked for me:

Subconscious Mind – My memories are stored with angry, happy, or sad emotions. When my subconscious mind speaks to me, these same emotions are attached to the memories. Thus, whenever the emotions of anger, sadness, or happiness accompany an idea, I know it's coming from my subconscious mind.

Imaginative Mind – Whenever I start thinking about future possibilities, I get excited and/or anxious. It's this excitement or anxiety that tells me I'm operating in my imaginative mind at the moment. If it's really exciting or if I'm really anxious or fearful, it's really my imagination.

Rational Mind – My rational mind is very good at pointing out all my real or potential faults. It tells me all the bad things about me and my ideas. So if any thought is critical of me in any way, or just a little bit cynical, I know that's my rational mind doing its thing. I usually feel the negative energy.

None of these minds or feelings is intuitive.

My intuitive mind is calm and peaceful. It never finds fault with me and it doesn't tell me what to do. It accepts me for who and what I am. It never volunteers any information about me unless I ask first. Then it encourages me to look at the things I like about me and enhance them. It asks me to look at the things I don't like about me and decide how to change them myself. It will give me suggestions when I ask but never unsolicited criticisms or analysis.

My intuitive mind is a master counselor who helps me identify what I want to do about me. It's a master teacher who leads me to opportunities for learning whenever I ask for help. It's a spiritual center for me where I can always find acceptance, peace, and quiet anytime, anywhere.

My intuitive mind answers my questions calmly and unemotionally. It tells me I have the power to change my own life, to change who and what I am, to become a better and more loving individual. It never tells me I am unsatisfactory or "bad."

My intuitive mind tunes into the subconscious minds of others to share information with me they want to share. It never violates another person's right to share or not at their discretion. But it does warn me when negative energy is being directed toward me. These things, I find, are also quite normal and to be expected as we open our "third eye" which we also call our intuitive mind.

As you continue to experience this calm and peaceful place within, you'll begin to hear the small, silent voice that is your intuition. It happens just as naturally as all of your bodily functions. In the beginning, these fleeting intuitive moments may take a long time to manifest.

The more you practice, the sooner you reach your intuitive mind and the longer you're able to remain there. As you continue to practice, you'll be able to move into your intuition in seconds. You'll be able to function there while doing other things such as talking, sleeping, working, or playing. You can stay tuned in and listen to your own small, silent voice anytime, anywhere.

This too is quite normal.

## 5

Some people contact their intuitive mind and receive a flow of information about life and things. The ideas just keep coming. It's as though somebody turned on the faucet and left the water running.

At least this is what happens in the beginning. The more you don't do anything about the knowledge you're gaining, the slower the ideas come until they just stop. It's as though somebody turned off the faucet. What you don't use, you lose.

That's a fact of life. If you don't use your muscles, they atrophy and lose strength. If you don't use your mind, it atrophies and you lose cognition. If you don't use your intuition, it stops talking.

Some people want their intuitive mind to be quiet so they can attain a state of Zen. So, they don't do anything about their intuitive insights while they're meditating. Other people want to encourage intuitive insights. So they write them down and do something about them. All of them. There's a third group of people who want to do both: to meditate for spiritual enlightenment and to receive intuitive insights. This is the more difficult path because you need to train your intuitive mind to know when you want to do what.

Decide how you want to use your intuitive mind. Write it all down in your journal. Then approach your intuitive mind with the expectation it will do exactly what you want it to do. It will. It will do what you instruct it to do. It will answer your questions or it will be as quiet as you wish.

## 6

Several people in the class that originally received these lectures asked questions, but all the questions seemed to center upon three themes:

QUESTION – How can I really tell if it's my intuition or my imagination?
  ANSWER – Your intuitive mind is unemotional. It's neutral and doesn't judge anything as good or bad. Your intuitive mind is non-assertive. It never gets aggressive or urges you to do something.

Your imaginative mind is emotional. It asserts itself and dominates your thoughts. More than anything, your imaginative mind is excited about what you're thinking. It judges things as good or bad and encourages us accordingly.

As a rule, if your thoughts are calm and peaceful, that could be your intuition. But if your thoughts are exciting and energetic, it can't be your intuitive mind that's speaking. The other thing is you'll always have a peaceful "knowing" when it's your intuitive mind that's speaking.

QUESTION – How do you know your imagination is always the future? Can't you imagine the past?
  ANSWER – As a rule, our imagination takes us into our possible futures and our subconscious mind accurately remembers our past. But, yes, we can play tricks on ourselves and imagine false memories. We can also imagine other possibilities than what actually happened. Mystics would argue these imaginings are possible future events in our lives.
QUESTION – How does intuition manifest in different people?
  ANSWER – Good question. Intuition manifests as our sixth sense as clairsentience (knowing) and this is attributed to the

element Spirit. But it can also manifest as a higher vibra-
tion of any of our five senses. These five higher senses are:
Clairvoyance (sight) [Fire]
Clairaudience (sound) [Water]
Clairodorance (smelling) [Air]
Clairgustance (taste) [Air]
Clairtangence (touch) [Earth]

The notes inside the square brackets are my own theories about
the dominant element working through the individual at that time.
It seems clairodorance and clairgustance come together most of the
time. The others seem to appear separately one at a time.

As human beings we have two higher minds which reside above our
intuition. Think of these three minds as a three-layer wedding cake. Our
intuitive mind forms the base of this cake. The top layer is our receptive
mind and in between is our conscience. Above this three-tier cake and
surrounding it in all directions forever is the mind of the Divine. How
insignificant our little receptive mind seems to be!

But the ancients called this the Mouth of the Divine and the considered it the most precious thing in the Divine's creation. For this is
the mouth through which the Divine speaks individually to each of us.
All we have to do is become receptive and receive.

What we receive from the Divine we filter through our conscience.
This is our free will. This is where we decide what's right or wrong
for us. This is where we corrupt the "Word of the Divine" and turn it
around for our own purposes. What we send to the Divine we send
through this filter and it filters out all the negativity, deceit, deception,
untruth, and falsehood that's in us. The truth is we can deceive ourselves, and we do it all the time, but our conscience won't let us deceive
our Maker. But that's OK because the Divine accepts us for who and
what we are just as parents accept their own children. But this is theol-
ogy and we won't go there.

We can travel through our intuitive mind into our conscience and
observe our five lower minds at work. We can see our corporeal mind
(unconscious) controlling our body. We can read our history (the akashic
record) in our subconscious mind. We can follow the threads of count-
less futures in our imagination. We can watch our rational mind solve
the problems of our life. And, we can see the faultless activity of our
intuitive mind.

We can see all these things and we can also look up and see our receptive mind connected to the universe. We can look up and see the abyss, the void, the Mouth of the Divine. (Some say what we're actually seeing is our own third eye.) Here in our conscience we can change the attitudes that color our concept of right and wrong. We can remove our prejudices and we can learn to love unconditionally. We can be "reborn" as a new person.

We can float up into our receptive mind and become "enlightened." We can "know" the Divine. We can watch the Divine Light flowing down through the Mouth of the Divine, nurturing our mind and body and flowing out through us back into the universe. We can learn to control that light. But that's another discussion for another time.

The ultimate answer to the question: "How do we know we're in our intuitive mind instead of our imagination?" is "Go to your conscience and you'll know." Looking down from above you can see how all of your lower minds are working and what each one is doing. The goal of meditation is enlightenment and that's attained when you reach your receptive mind. The universal rule governing this is that you will ultimately attain that which you seek. Just keep seeking.

For now, practice meditation, open your intuitive mind and use it. That's the path to spiritual enlightenment and it's the path to communing with the Divine.

CHAPTER 9

# How to *really* learn tarot

*1*

In my opinion, the number one cause of difficulty in learning the meanings of the tarot cards, for most students, is they have too many definitions for each card.

Have you ever heard a reader tell somebody this card means such and such, and then proceed to give a number of alternative meanings? I have. It drives me nuts. It's like a multiple choice test. Select the best answer. Select any answer. Select anything. The reader is always right if there are enough choices to cover all contingencies.

This card means somebody in your life is going to get pregnant. But it can also mean a change at work or a career change. If you're getting close to somebody, they're not ready to make a commitment. If you don't have anybody yet, this card means a new man's coming into your life—but not real soon. It also means new ideas coming to you. If you plan on taking a vacation soon, this card says you'll have a good time. Yes, but what's the real answer?

The real answer is this reader is unsure of him- or herself and doesn't believe his or her cards yet. I mean, how could little colored pieces of paper with pretty pictures painted on them tell us anything?

The truth is they can't. Tarot cards can't tell us anything by them-selves. They need to be interpreted, and that's where we come in.

Here's how tarot works in my opinion:

1. We decide what each card is going to mean. We make a conscious decision this card is going to mean this. We can base this decision on our experience, the things we've read, the things we see in the card, or our gut feeling. But whatever we do, the first step is for us to decide what each card means.

2. We communicate these meanings to our subconscious minds. This is the easy part. Our subconscious mind remembers everything. The problem is we forget. So to solve that problem, write down the meanings you decided upon in the first step. If you forget, you can look them up. Your subconscious mind never forgets. So the second step is to write down your decisions from step one. This act alone lets your subconscious mind know you're serious about your decision.

3. Your subconscious mind takes over from there and arranges the tarot pack in such a manner that exactly the right card will come up in the perfect position to answer the question at hand. This will happen regardless of who shuffles the cards, and regardless of how the cards are shuffled, cut, and selected. I used to believe it was important to shuffle, cut, and select the cards in a certain manner. I'm now con-vinced it makes absolutely no difference how you shuffle, cut, and select the cards. Your subconscious mind will control the operation no matter what you do. In other words, the reading will be right in spite of you. So all you have to do is the first two steps: 1) define each card, and 2) write it down.

The first secret to really learning how to use tarot is to define each card with one and only one meaning. It doesn't matter what that meaning is. It can be a word, a phrase, a concept, anything. It can be something in the card or not. It can be something you know or something somebody else knows. You can use any system you want to use. Just decide on one meaning for each card and write it down.

From now on, whenever your subconscious mind wants to convey to you exactly that meaning, it will select that card and present it to you in your reading. In my opinion, that's how it all works.

## Questions and answers

Q – Doesn't it really limit you if you can only use one word for a definition of each tarot card?

A – Yes, it does and that's the idea. The better you define each card
the better your communication with your own subconscious mind.
If you have four definitions for each card, how do you know which
one to use? The truest answer is you don't unless you build a system to do just that.

What I'm proposing is just that kind of a system for reading tarot cards.
The first step is to decide upon one key word, phrase, or concept for
each tarot card. The second step is to learn to use that set of seventy-
eight meanings to do tarot readings. The rest of the steps to be explained
in the chapters of this book will explain how to use up to four different
meanings with each card. That's the system being proposed.

Read about it and then build your own system for reading tarot
cards. That's my recommendation.

Q – Can you give us some definitions for the problem cards?

A – Not really. My experience is that different people have difficulty
defining different cards. Every card in the pack is a problem card for
somebody. If you ever have a card which you just can't define for
some reason, here's a few suggestions:

1. Look at the card. Really study it. Look at your list of possible
   meanings derived from a number of authors. Look at the card.
   Repeat this process until something clicks for you.

2. Take up your thesaurus and look up all the words on your list.
   Select as many potential new words from your thesaurus as possible. Write them all down. You can even look up some of the
   new words for additional possibilities. Use this new expanded
   list to repeat the first suggestion. If you don't have a thesaurus
   you can find one in the reference section of your local library.

3. Look at the card. What's happening in the card? Describe what's
   happening in the card and select your key word, phrase, or concept for that card.

4. Look at the symbols in the card. What do these symbols mean
   to you? Use these symbol meanings to select your key word,
   phrase, or concept.

5. Consider the number of the card. What does this number mean to you? Then consider the suit of the card. What does this suit mean to you? Using this information write down a key word, phrase, or concept.

6. Meditate on the card and/or contemplate the card until you intuit a key word, phrase, or concept for that card.

7. Ask your higher self, angels, or spirit guides for assistance.

Your first assignment is to eliminate all but one meaning for each of your cards. Select a word, phrase, or concept and write it down so both you and your subconscious mind agree on that meaning. Your subconscious mind always agrees with you, so make a decision. Your subconscious mind will agree.

## 2

The largest group of problems that stymie beginning tarot readers is that they second-guess themselves.

Having looked at a card and having decided what that card means, the reader starts to hedge his or her bets by adding additional meanings to the card. One of my good friends calls this the "badge of an apprentice."

Apprentices in any field strive to be right. The perception is that if they're right they're learning the trade. In my experience we don't learn a whole lot by always being right. We learn through our mistakes. The problem is that we're often right the first time and we're wrong every guess after that.

The more we prattle on, the more wrong we are. We should be learning a lot. But unfortunately, most of us don't know it's a mistake to keep guessing. In the previous section of this chapter, my suggestion for avoiding this problem was to select one and only one key word, phrase, or concept for each tarot card.

When you start second-guessing yourself, all you need to do is remind yourself of the meaning you've assigned to that card. The discussion in your head is over. You know the answer.

The second largest group of problems that keep beginners from learning tarot is forgetting the question to be answered. They ask the question, select the cards and talk about the cards but not about how the cards answer the question at hand. In my opinion this has more to do with tarot spreads than tarot cards.

Based on my experience, most beginners fail to realize the power of a one-card tarot reading. Most of them believe using more cards results in a better reading. With a poor understanding of how to do one-card tarot readings, using more cards never solves the problem, they only add to the confusion. This is a situation where more is definitely not better.

For example, let's consider the ever-popular Mind-Body-Spirit tarot spread. I consider this as three simple one-card tarot spreads and read the cards accordingly. Here's how this process works using a made-up question:

Q – What does (the client) need to do in order to attract the right man into her life?

A – Using the Mind-Body-Spirit spread, I suggest the reader answer three questions:
   1. What does the client need to do intellectually (mentally) to attract the right man into her life?
   2. What does the client need to do physically to attract the right man into her life?
   3. What does the client need to do spiritually to attract the right man into her life?

Oh, wow, doesn't that make it easier? The three-card tarot spread turns out to be three one-card tarot readings. A spread of any length turns out to be that many one-card readings. That's a fascinating secret very few people really understand. Now you're one of them.

Notice that my reading of the first card didn't answer the whole question. The first card answered the first sub-question implied by the spread I chose to use. And it answered only the first implied sub-question. In effect, the first card only answers one-third of the question asked. That's what tarot spreads do. Tarot spreads subdivide the question asked into separate parts of the question. A one-card reading has one answer. It answers only one question. A ten-card reading has ten answers as ten separate sub-questions are being asked by a ten-card spread.

Each card answers only one implied sub-question. None of the ten cards answers the question directly, unless you have a position in your spread devoted to that purpose, the purpose of answering the question asked. This card is often called the "outcome" card if the question is about the outcome of a certain action.

In a Past-Present-Future tarot spread, only the Future card answers a question about a future event. By the same token, only the Present card answers a question about what's going on now. And, only the Past card can answer: "What happened?"

Your second assignment is to look at the tarot spreads you use and practice discovering the implied sub-questions for several questions you pose to the cards. You'll be amazed at how the quality of your readings improves by using this simple technique. If you use a five-card tarot spread, look for the five implied sub-questions and answer each of them. Now you have the five answers to the original question you expected using this spread. Have fun experimenting

### 3

If you've been doing the assignments you've accomplished the following two very important improvements to your tarot toolbox: 1. You've identified one key word, phrase, or concept for each card, and 2. You've increased your understanding about how to use a tarot spread. From here we'll concentrate on how to improve your overall approach to doing a tarot reading.

The third most common problem that hinders the development of good tarot readers is that they answer everything but the question posed by their client. I believe this is caused in part by numerous nebulous definitions for their cards and in part because they haven't developed good one-card tarot reading skills. The first two sections of this chapter addressed those two problems.

The rest of the story is that some readers get so caught up in the story they forget the question. If you address the implied sub-questions for each position in your tarot spread, you'll minimize this problem.

But if you'll summarize what you'v e already discovered from these focused one-card readings, you'll eliminate this problem altogether. Take the example we used in the previous section:

Q – What does (the client) need to do in order to attract the right man into her life?

A – Using the Mind-Body-Spirit spread, I suggest the reader answer three questions:

1. What does the client need to do intellectually (mentally) to attract the right man into her life?
2. What does the client need to do physically to attract the right man into her life?
3. What does the client need to do spiritually to attract the right man into her life? Now I have three answers to three questions. All that's left is to relate these answers to the original question. It can be done in three sentences in this manner: You need to mentally (blank) in order to attract the right man into your life. You need to physically (blank) in order to attract the right man into your life. You need to (blank) spiritually in order to attract the right man into your life. Blank is the answer you received for each sub-question in the reading.

This summary is the conclusion of the reading. The only thing left is to ask your client if he or she has any questions about this reading. If your client does have a question, you can either answer it with the cards before you or draw an additional "clarification" card.

As you can see, this system is very logical. It has several purposes and three of those purposes are to resolve the four largest problems that hinder prospective tarot readers from becoming tarot readers. We've just discussed the first three. The fourth is that readers don't know how to do one-card tarot readings. You can find some excellent resources addressing this topic in the previous chapters. Your third assignment is to practice answering the implied sub-questions and the original question for several questions you pose to the cards. It's also a good idea to practice doing as many one-card tarot readings as you can.

# 4

My previous insights in this series identified three reasons people have problems learning and mastering tarot:

1. They have too many definitions for each card and get confused.
2. They have too many meanings for each position in a tarot spread.
3. They answer everything but the question asked.

The fourth problem that hinders the development of good tarot readers in my opinion is they don't know how to give a good one-card tarot reading. If the card they draw doesn't look like an answer to the question they posed, they panic. When they panic they do one of several things:

1. They answer a different question
2. They imaginatively interpret the card
3. They draw another card
4. They ask the same question again
5. They ask another question.

Probably the easiest thing to do when it looks like the card you picked doesn't answer your question is answer another question. It's easy to think the card is answering another question. You hear tarot readers justify this approach by saying the cards don't always answer the question you ask. Presumably the cards answer the most important question in your life at this time.

I don't believe that. I believe the cards always answer the question asked. Maybe we don't understand the answer. Maybe we don't want to hear the answer we're given. Maybe we doubt our ability to interpret the cards. Been there, done all of that. Now I believe the cards always give me the best possible answer. Here's an example from my memory bank:

My client asked me when she'd meet her true love. I drew the Nine of Swords which meant "An ending of new ideas." I stared at that card knowing its meaning, and also knowing that wasn't an answer to her question at all. My imagination traveled all over the place. I was looking for any explanation and my mind was blank. My client interrupted my racing mind by noting the card looked like an unhappy ending and my panic increased. I responded with some inane comment like: "Well, it's not as bad as it looks."

You've got to know I was in trouble with this reading. I was panicked—pure panic. So she asked the obvious: "What does it mean?" I searched my mind for answers and found none. I let my imagination loose. Still nothing. The look on her face told me to say something so I said something like: "The Swords are mental cards. They talk about thinking, new ideas, and new concepts. But the Nine of Swords is an ending to this process. It says that as soon as you stop coming up with all these thoughts and new ideas, the love you seek will enter your life."

Thankfully I shut up and started searching my mind for more answers. I was thinking about telling her the cards don't always answer the question we ask but they always give us important information.

I was thinking about telling her that in this situation the card meant something different. I was still thinking about what something different the card was telling her, when she said: "That makes sense."

Makes sense? It made absolutely no sense to me whatsoever.

That particular client developed into a really fine tarot reader. I never think of her without thinking about how the cards always give the right answer whether we understand it or not. We both learned something in that tarot reading. I daresay I learned the most.

My suggestion to you any time you have a card that doesn't appear to answer the question, is to go back to the basics. Write down the question. Write down the card drawn and its meaning. Tell yourself or your client what this card usually means. Then find out how that answer applies to your life or the life of your client. I call this process "interpreting the cards."

I believe one tarot card will always answer one question. We just have to keep going back to the definition of the card to see how it answers the question. Then we have to interpret this answer so it makes sense to our client. Unless we just happen to be our own client, it doesn't matter if it makes any sense to us or not.

You'll be surprised at how often you'll be able to answer your client's questions, and not understand the answer yourself, if you just stick to the meanings you've assigned to your tarot cards. It happens to me all the time. I'm in the dark. My client understands the answer given by the cards. That's a good tarot reading in my book. It matters only that my client understands the reading.

Since the cards always answer the question asked, there's no need for panic and no need for the alternatives used by panicked readers. There's no need for additional cards, repetitions of questions, or other imaginative techniques. But you can always have a backup strategy in case you need it.

Your fourth assignment is to practice answering all kinds of questions with one-card draws.

## 5

The fifth problem that prospective tarot readers face that keeps them from becoming good tarot readers is they allow their imagination to take over instead of their intuition. This is easy enough to prevent if you pay attention to your readings. First of all, if you've defined your cards so you know what each card means, you'll know when your imagination wants to play. You'll look at the card and imagine it means something else.

But you know that's not true, because you know what that card really means to you. At this point, you can smile to yourself, thank your imagination, and ask it to go play somewhere else for awhile. Notice the sound of your imagination. It always sounds a lot like you. It usually can be easily heard above the clamor of your mind, and sometimes it's even rather loud. It has an emotional quality about itself and you feel this energy as much as you hear it in your mind.

Imaginations usually tell us things, sometimes order us around, and generally show a lot of self-confidence. They usually barge right in any time and say what they want to say.

Our intuitive mind is gentler and softer. It never tells us what to do. It's never emotional about anything and there's no emotional energy around it. It always speaks in a soft voice and it sounds like somebody else rather than you. Besides, intuition usually speaks so softly we can't identify who it sounds like anyway. In my experience, intuition is also rather introverted.

Our intuitive mind would never tell us to change the meaning of a card during a reading. Never.

In the first place, intuition suggests and never orders. Second, it builds upon what we already know. It adds to the meaning of a card rather than changing the meaning during a reading. On the other hand, when we're meditating with our cards, our intuition may suggest different meanings for us to consider. Remember, intuition always suggests and never orders us to do anything.

# 6

This suggestion is probably a little obvious, but you'd be surprised at how many potentially good tarot readers fall into one or more of the following traps and never recover:

Trap 1 – The tarot reader uses too many tarot decks. It's confusing to learn to read tarot cards using more than one deck. The more decks you try to use in the beginning the more confusing it becomes. Learn to use one tarot deck very well and learning the second deck and subsequent decks will be easier.

Trap 2 – The tarot reader uses too many tarot spreads. It's hard to learn and remember more than one tarot spread and consistently do it well. Trying to learn and remember two or more spreads is difficult. Learn to use one tarot spread very well in the beginning and other spreads will be easier to learn later.

My personal suggestion is to learn to do one-card tarot readings very well before you start using multiple-card tarot spreads. Then use three-card or five-card spreads before trying the Celtic Cross.

Trap 3 – The tarot reader spends too little time with his or her tarot cards. The more you look at, meditate with, and study your tarot cards, the better. Small chunks of time every day is better than one large chunk once a week, in my opinion. If you only have a few minutes, study a small group of cards each day.

My suggestion is to study one rank a day for fourteen days and Keys XV through XXI on the fifteenth day. When studying the ranks, you'll have five cards each day: the Major Arcana (Key) and four cards in the Minor Arcana of the same rank. Use Page = 11, Knight = 12, Queen = 13, and King = 14 for the court cards. Look at the cards, repeat their meanings, and momentarily picture them in your mind throughout the day. It only takes a few minutes each morning.

Trap 4 – The tarot reader pays too much attention to what others say and not enough to his or her own intuitive insights and subconscious mind. What others say works for them. Find out what works best for you. If somebody has a good idea you want to use, use it. Otherwise, use your own biases and preferences. Learn tarot your way. The quicker you decide to do it your way, the faster you'll become a good tarot reader.

# CHAPTER 10

# The seven-day tarot spread

Choose a day of the week to start your seven-day tarot spread. My personal preference is Sunday, but you may choose any day of the week. My reason for choosing Sunday is my work week runs from Monday through Friday. Sunday evening is the time for me to plan the next five days. This is my time for setting goals and determining objectives and getting ready for the week to follow.

Choose a time of the day to start your seven-day tarot spread. My personal preference is in the evening after things have settled down. This is a good time for me to become calm and centered. I relax, let the cares of the world go away, and enter into a reflective and receptive state of mind. That's a good time for me to start my seven-day tarot spread.

Select a card that sets the tone for your spiritual purpose for the following week. This card may be selected in any manner you choose. My preference is to fan the deck and ask the question: "What's the most important lesson for me to learn this week?" By holding my hand over the fanned deck, I'm able to sense which card is to be chosen as an answer for my question. You may use any method of selection you desire and ask any question you want to ask. The idea is to choose a time and place to start your seven-day tarot spread. Choose a question for the week, one you'll ask daily seven more times. Your question for each day will ask the question for that day only. The same question will be used for the week and for each day of the week. A little rephrasing may be required.

Study the card you've selected for the coming week. Write down your question, the name of this card, the meaning of this card, and the answer to your question. That's the way I like to do it. By writing it all down I have less of a tendency to bend things around later to suit my mood. The point is to determine what is the true answer to your question. This answer tells you what you need to know for the whole week.

My suggestion is to leave this card out in a prominent place where you'll see it every day for the next seven days. I have it sitting out on my desk at home with a small piece of cloth covering it when I'm gone. It's right there in the middle of my desk where I can't help but see it. The temptation to look at it is overwhelming. So I look whenever the opportunity arises. Even when it's covered I can see the card in my mind's eye.

Later that evening you can use a visualization of that card to help you fall asleep. This gives you the opportunity to review the possibilities for learning experiences every day for the next week.

The following morning, visit your deck, look at the card, and ask your question again, but rephrase it not for the week but for today. My usual question is: "What's the most important thing for me to learn today?" I go through my usual procedures and select my card for the day. This card I place not beside, but below the first card. This will be the first card in a row of seven cards which I'll place side by side below my card for the week.

My procedure is to write down my daily question, the name of the card drawn, the meaning of this card, and my reading for the day. Keep in mind, this reading is a part of the reading for the whole week, it's not separate from the reading you started the day before. It's a part of the whole reading you're going to create day by day this week.

Continue this process for the next six days which will take you back to the day you started this reading. The seven-day tarot spread starts and ends on the same day of the week. On that day you'll have one card above a row of seven cards. The card above is the answer to your question for the week. The seven cards in the row below answer your seven daily questions for the same week. A total of eight cards are used in the spread.

As you read the card for each day, you might take a few moments to reflect on how this card fits into the big picture for the week. You can do this by looking at all the cards already in the spread. Write it all down. Keep a running record and check it often.

A variation of the seven-day tarot spread that has a lot of merit is to consciously choose the card for the week. Say you want to learn about imagination this week. Choose the card you feel most closely defines what you want to learn. Place this card at the top of the spread. In my case this would be the Empress who in my system is the fruitful queen of imagination. In your system, you choose the card you want to choose.

Another variation I like to use is to work through the Major Arcana one card a week asking what that card is teaching you now about itself. For example, if this were the week for the Empress, my question might be: "How can I use my imagination to my advantage this week?" Each day I'll be asking: "How can I use my imagination to my advantage today?"

One Sunday evening I asked the question: "What's the most important thing for me to learn this week?" I drew the Judgement card. In my system, this card means "rebirth." This is a process of becoming reborn, or born again. My reading of this card was: "The most important thing for me to learn this week is how to rebirth myself into the person I'd like to become."

Monday morning my card was the Ten of Wands. In my system this is the Fire expression of Key X which means: "What goes around, comes around" as it relates to my intentions (Fire). Good! I will learn what I intend to learn. I will learn what I intend for others to learn. I will learn what I intend to teach others. My reading: The most important thing for me to learn today is what I intend to teach to others. This will help me become the person I want to become.

Tuesday morning my card was the Hierophant which means intuition in my system. My reading: The most important thing for me to learn today is to use my intuition. I will use my intuition to help me rebirth myself and to help me identify what I want to teach others. Notice how this card relates to both the card for yesterday and the card for the week. This is how the seven-day tarot reading works.

Wednesday morning my card was the Ace of Wands which is the Fire expression of The Magician (all aces relate to The Magician by number). The Magician means: "Pay Attention." Wands are intentions. The Ace means to pay attention to my intentions. In the system I'm using,

Fire is intentions, Water is relationships, Air is thoughts, and Earth is the body. Reversed, Fire is career, Water is emotions, Air is attitudes, and Earth is money. The number of the pip card relates to the card in the Major Arcana with the same number. Pages are eleven, Knights twelve, Queens thirteen and Kings fourteen. The Major Arcana depict a spiritual journey. Reversed cards of the Major Arcana represent the same spiritual journey but indicate a spiritual hang-up or blockage, a spiritual issue or problem.

To continue, my reading of the Ace of Wands is: I need to pay attention to my intentions today to help me rebirth myself. I can rely on my intuition (yesterday's card) and I do need to be concerned about what I intend to teach others (Monday's card).

Thursday morning my card was the Five of Wands which means intuiting (Hierophant is Five) my intentions (Wands is Fire and Fire is intentions). The first thing I notice is a repetition of "intentions" and "intuition." I really need to pay attention (Magician and Aces) to my intentions (Wands) and intuition (Hierophant and Fives). The message for the week is pretty clear at this point. Anyway, that was my reading for the day.

Friday morning my card was the reversed Death card. To me this card means to change my behavior. Reversed it means this is a spiritual issue for me. It's not just a simple tap on the shoulder, it's a message that something's wrong and some behavior needs changing.

At this point, let me digress. The message for the week is fairly well answered and it was coming through loud and clear. The message for Friday gave me pause to reconsider how I had been implementing my intentions for rebirthing myself into the person I want to become. Then it hit me. It was more of a Tower experience than a rainbow.

I had received several intuitive hints about how to change the curriculum I was rewriting. But the fact is I was discounting those intuitive hints (that's easy for me to do) and sticking with the standard "time-proven" approach. Tradition was winning out over innovation. You don't rebirth yourself by doing the same old things over and over again. Death paid me a visit on that day to tell me I have a spiritual problem and need to change my behavior. If I really want to rebirth myself I need to pay attention to my intuitive insights and my intentions.

Saturday morning my card was the reversed Three of Wands. Three is the Empress and she relates to imagination. My key phrase for the Empress is Imagine the Possibilities. Reversed Wands relate to career.

My career right now is writing curriculum, articles, reviews, and newsletters. My reading for the week is only slightly modified by Saturday's reading. The message is to imagine the possibilities for my career, change my behavior, pay attention to my intentions, and use my intuition. By doing these things I'll rebirth myself into the person I want to become.

Sunday morning my card was the Justice card which means things are the way they're supposed to be. In looking back over the seven-day spread I could see how things were actually changing in my life. I left this spread out for the remainder of the day.

Toward evening I felt I'd learned the lesson I was supposed to learn. The message was I was making progress, I was changing my behavior, I was paying attention to my intentions, I was allowing my intuitive insights to influence my writing. I was in the process of rebirthing myself into the person I intend to become. I picked up the cards and shuffled them back into the pack. After several minutes, I posed a question to the deck and started the whole process all over again.

The seven-day tarot spread is just that. It takes seven days to complete the spread and it speaks about the week in progress. You can spend a couple of minutes a day with your seven-day tarot spread or you can spend longer. You can do it at home and forget it or you can carry it in your head with you throughout the day. You can use it to help yourself along your spiritual path or you can use it for any purpose you decide. I hope you find a purpose that works for you.

# INDEX

Printed in the USA
CPSIA information can be obtained
at www.ICGtesting.com
JSHW012138021024
70951JS00017B/617